LITERARY CONCORDANCES

Other titles of interest

AINSWORTH
Mechanisms of Speech Recognition

BATAILLE
A Turning Point for Literacy

BEECH and FRANSELLA
Research and Experiment in Stuttering

BOLTON
Concept Formation

CHAPMAN
The Process of Learning Mathematics

LOWE and LOWE
On Teaching Foreign Languages to Adults

RABEN
Computer Assisted Research in Humanities

RICHARDS
The Language of Reason

LITERARY CONCORDANCES

*A Guide to the Preparation of
Manual and Computer Concordances*

by

T. H. HOWARD-HILL

Professor of English, University of South Carolina, USA

PERGAMON PRESS

OXFORD • NEW YORK • TORONTO • PARIS • SYDNEY • FRANKFURT

U.K.	Pergamon Press Ltd., Headington Hill Hall, Oxford OX3 0BW, England
U.S.A.	Pergamon Press Inc., Maxwell House, Fairview Park, Elmsford, New York 10523, U.S.A.
CANADA	Pergamon of Canada, Suite 104, 150 Consumers Road, Willowdale, Ontario M2 J1P9, Canada
AUSTRALIA	Pergamon Press (Aust.) Pty. Ltd., P.O. Box 544, Potts Point, N.S.W. 2011, Australia
FRANCE	Pergamon Press SARL. 24 rue des Ecoles, 75240 Paris, Cedex 05, France
FEDERAL REPUBLIC OF GERMANY	Pergamon Press GmbH, 6242 Kronberg-Taunus, Pferdstrasse 1, Federal Republic of Germany

First edition 1979

British Library Cataloguing in Publication Data

Howard-Hill, Trevor Howard
Literary concordances.
1. Concordances — Data processing — Standards
I. Title
801'.959   Z695.92   78-40568

ISBN 0-08-023021-0

Printed and bound in Great Britain by
William Clowes (Beccles) Limited, Beccles and London

CONTENTS

LIST OF FIGURES

PREFACE

AS THE following discussion of the form and arrangement of literary concordances was originally written for presentation at the International Conference on Literary Computing held at Oxford in April 1976, an intention which was frustrated by the paper's burgeoning extent, the tone is possibly not congenial to publication in its present form. Notwithstanding, I hope readers will bear the occasion in mind and join with me, albeit remotely, in grappling with complexities which do not frequently yield to graceful forms of expression.

My indebtedness to my friend and colleague, Dr. Robert L. Oakman, already considerable for conversations and stimulation over past years, is appreciably increased by the technical appendix on the concordance generator COCOA which he has generously provided. Deficiencies of the present examination of concordances are compensated for in his forthcoming *Computer Methods for Literary Research* (University of South Carolina Press).

Columbia, S.C.   T.H. HOWARD-HILL

CHAPTER 1

INTRODUCTION

MANY years ago in Oxford when I advised the Clarendon Press about literary computing, an assistant professor wrote from an American university proposing to concord the whole of world literature. Clearly he wanted something fairly impressive in his dossier for the Tenure Committee. The Press, he had no doubt, would publish the fruits of his industry. Had the Press agreed to the proposition it is quite likely that the task would be accomplished by now, but they didn't and it isn't. Despite the impression one receives from the constant flow of computer-generated concordances from the world's presses, there remains much to be done: there is little likelihood that scholars will cease to need, and produce, concordances to authors whose works are worthy of the labours necessary to concord them — and many to authors whose works are not. Consequently, there is room in the literature for a modest examination of the form and arrangement of literary concordances which can draw from the leading examples of past years in order to determine the considerations which might best govern the production of new concordances.

Whoever sets out to make a concordance finds only a few articles which offer general guidance, and those technical introductions to published concordances which supply the most useful details of concording techniques are usually silent about the reasons which impel the concordance editor to prefer one method of arrangement to another. Now that the prospective concordance editor yields a great part of the drudgery of concording to the slavish computer, and thereby relinquishes the opportunity to learn about concording directly by hard-won experience, it is all the more necessary to acquire a sound understanding of the principles of concording, i.e. those general considerations which influence the host of decisions about particular

1

matters which the editor must make.[1] If he does not make them, his computer programmer or a standard concordance programme will make them for him, to the detriment of his function as an editor. In short, the concordance editor must understand what he intends to accomplish before he approaches the computer, for only with a thorough grasp of concording principles will he be able to resist the blandishments of those who will attempt to persuade him, often in impressively technical language, that what he wants cannot be accomplished.

I do not wish to give the impression that concording is difficult in itself: the complexities which a prospective concordance editor might encounter will arise from the complexity of his basic material, the literary text, in whatever language it be written, and not from the concording process itself. Even with texts like the masques of Ben Jonson — to which I refer in detail later — the concordance editor can simply cut, Gordian-wise, through the complexities of typography, language, subordination of text, notes and glosses and the like, with a basic concordance programme. On the other hand, there are short texts in modern orthography in connection with which the kinds of problems which will be discussed shortly simply will not arise, and a reader with that kind of text need go no further here. However, for the purposes of discussion I refer by and large to difficult cases, and in the main am concerned to decide what the best method or solution for a problem of concording might be, disregarding the practicalities of a local computing environment. After all, if an editor cannot obtain the facilities to undertake the kind of concordance arrangement he considers desirable, there is nothing to be done — he must do his best with what he has. Nevertheless, it is important to notice that the editor's intention to publish his concordance, and thereby subject his work to more than private use and criticism, significantly influences the structure of the concordance. Essentially a concordance prepared for a single user need come under no broader rubric: no principles or conventions of concording need bind him should he not desire to acknowledge them. The contrary is true, however, as I show later, when a concordance is intended for public use. Therefore, the main topic here is published concordances, and, because the limitations of one's own education and interests are not readily escaped, concordances to texts in the English language.

The Concordance

It is necessary first to distinguish the concordance from two other index arrangements which are often associated with the concordance and sometimes, indeed, confused with it, because of their common functions (Fig. 1).

Verbal Index

The first is the verbal index (*index verborum* in Latin) which supplies an alphabetical list of the words (types) in a text corpus and references to those parts of the text where the individual occurrences (tokens) of the word may be found. Montgomery's "concordance" to Dryden is a good example of the verbal index, an arrangement which is favoured when an author is especially voluminous or the indexer unable for whatever reason to provide illustrative contexts as well as text references.

The Concordance

This differs essentially from the verbal index only in that the use of each token is illustrated by a quotation drawn from the text. The arrangement and display of the contexts may be simple or elaborate, as later discussion will show, and the concordance editor may provide a number of additional features which, so long as contexts are given, will not affect the index's status as a concordance.

The Lexicon

However, if homonymic and polysemantic homographs are distinguished, and if inflected forms are listed under a lemma, then the concordance becomes a dictionary or lexicon to which considerations apply which far exceed the scope of this paper. Nevertheless, some attention is paid to lemmatization in a subsequent section where the significant differences between the concordance and dictionaries appear clearly.

The basic function of a concordance is to bring together ("concord") passages of text which illustrate the use of a word — however "word" might be defined. If the passages are not brought together but are merely referred to, then one has a verbal index; if the passages, having been brought together, are rearranged and subordinated according to their philological or other relationships, then the product is a lexicon or special concordance of the kind discussed in Chapter 8. The general position adopted here is that the concordance is a general-purpose working tool for the study of literature. Although there are a number of additional features which might enhance the concordance's usefulness for different kinds of literary and linguistic study, abandonment of the simple alphabetical arrangement of headings — to which all users have equally easy access — in favour of more sophisticated arrangements designed to facilitate specialized applications of the index necessarily restricts the general usefulness of the concordance. My topic here is the concordance prepared for publication and consequently intended for dissemination amongst scholars of diverse aims and competencies, concordances which, very often, will be the first and last undertaken for the individual author or work. For his own research the concordance editor will naturally arrange and rearrange his materials as best suits the nature of his own investigations. When concordances enter the public area through publication, however, I take it as axiomatic that their arrangement should assist the widest possible use.[2] The responsibility of the concordances is general and comprehensive rather than specialized and exclusive.

The editor of a concordance intended for publication has, at a time when the handmade concordance is proclaimed dead,[3] to concern himself with a large number of detailed technical matters related to data preparation, coding, pre-editing, computer facilities, input and output and the like which will not be discussed here. Although published accounts of successful concordance enterprises will supply him with specific guides and general advice, the concordancer will find that much of the technical information has been rendered obsolete by the revolution of the times, that he will not have access to many of the facilities described in the more recent literature, that funds for the support of concordances are increasingly difficult to obtain, and that after he has laboured to prepare his text for computation, his computing

```
GLENMALURE -------------- (1)   211/08
GLIBLY ------------------ (1)   241/10
GLIMMER ----------------- (4)   111/26
  112/02  170/13  172/31
GLIMMERED --------------- (1)   244/08
GLIMMERING -------------- (3)   087/03
  141/01  172/31
GLIMPSE ----------------- (3)   064/09
  120/09  178/28
GLIMPSES ---------------- (1)   062/21
GLINT ------------------- (1)   206/01
GLISTENING -------------- (1)   029/29
GLITTERED --------------- (1)   137/34
GLOAT ------------------- (1)   133/04
GLOBUM ------------------ (1)   198/03
GLOOM ------------------- (11)  055/30
  058/13  068/09  299/36  135/06  136/04
  143/16  147/16  148/36  188/03  244/22
GLOOMILY ---------------- (2)   070/07
  240/29
GLOOMY ------------------ (7)   066/03
  068/29  077/24  107/08  114/30  190/36
  232/23
GLORIAM ----------------- (2)   056/01
  108/12
GLORIES ----------------- (2)   104/32
  152/16
GLORIFIED --------------- (1)   240/05
GLORIOSI ---------------- (1)   210/07
GLORIOUS ---------------- (3)   107/32
  113/17  148/23
GLORY ------------------- (5)   134/02
  138/31  172/12  186/23  210/07
GLOSSY ------------------ (1)   084/22
GLOVES ------------------ (1)   064/13
GLOW -------------------- (19)  017/18
  021/20  038/28  073/08  078/07  108/21
  125/08  155/16  161/23  161/24  163/09
  163/13  166/29  217/29  218/01  219/27
  219/36  222/02  223/07
GLOWED ------------------ (1)   173/02
GLOWERING --------------- (1)   106/14
GLOWING ----------------- (8)   027/32
  038/28  075/27  105/11  121/31  122/13
  142/28  166/36
GLUTTONOUS -------------- (1)   106/13
GLUTTONY ---------------- (1)   144/10
GLYNN ------------------- (7)   235/17
  235/20  235/28  235/33  236/01  236/08
  236/31
GLYNN'S ----------------- (2)   235/19
  236/07
GNAWED ------------------ (1)   132/37
GNAWS ------------------- (2)   120/01
  130/06
GO ---------------------- (89)  009/17
  011/13  012/03  012/03  013/16  014/07
  017/11  018/26  018/29  019/04  022/19
```

Gnat, the insect Culex: Lucr. 1014. Err. II, 2, 20. Merch. III, 2, 123. John IV, 1, 93. H6C II, 6, 9. Tit. IV, 4, 82. Rom. I, 4, 64. Ant. III, 13, 166. Cymb. I, 3, 21. Per. II, 3, 62. *to see a king transformed to a g.* LLL IV, 3, 166 (cf. Per. II, 3, 62).

Gnaw (impf. —*ed,* R3 I, 4, 25; partic. *gnawn,* Wiv. II, 2, 307. 1) to tear off by slow corrosion with the fore teeth: H6A III, 1, 73. H6B III, 1, 192. R3 II, 4, 28. IV, 2, 27 (Qq *bites*). Cor. I, 1, 254. Tit. III, 1, 262. Tim. IV, 3, 49. Oth. V, 2, 43. With an accus. denoting the result: – *ing my bands in sunder,* Err. V, 243. Figuratively: *the thought doth like a poisonous mineral g. my inwards,* Oth. II, 1, 306. *hell g. his bones,* IV, 2, 136. Absol. *the —ing vulture of thy mind,* Tit. V, 2, 31.
2) intr.: *my reputation gnawn at,* Wiv. II, 2, 307. *men that fishes —ed upon,* R3 I, 4, 25.

Go (impf. *went;* partic. *gone;*) 1) to move step by step, to walk: *I never saw a goddess go,* Sonn. 30, 11. *as proper a man as ever went on four legs,* Tp. II, 2, 63. *I can go no farther,* III, 3, 1. *love will creep in service where it cannot go,* Gent. IV, 2, 20. *your wit ambles well, it – es easily,* Adv V, 1, 159. *I can no farther crawl, no farther go,* Mids. III, 2, 444. *if you go – No fair afront, I shall be weary,* H4A II, 3, 86. *cannot go but thirty mile a day,* H4B II, 4, 179. *ride more than thou – est,* Lr. I, 4, 134. – *ing shall be used with feet,* III, 2, 94.
2) to walk leisurely, not to run: *we'll not run, nor go neither.* Tp. III, 2, 22. *thou must run to him, for thou hast stayed so long that –ing will scarce serve the turn,* Gent. III, 1, 388.
3) to make haste: *towards thee I'll run, and give him leave to go,* Sonn. 51, 14. *trip and go,* LLL IV, 2, 145. *I go, I go, look how I go,* Mids. III, 2, 100. *run, go!* H6B III, 2, 55.
4) to depart (the opposite of to come): *all this service have I done since I went,* Tp. V, 226. *to-mo. row be in readiness to go,* Gent. 3, 3, 70. *is your countryman gone?* III, 2, 12. *my daughter takes his —ing grievously,* 14. *is the duke gone?* Mens. V, 301. *pluck but his name out of his heart, and turn him —ing.*

the sun shines, let foolish gnats make sport.	ERR	2.02	30
hearts of men | faster than gnats in cobwebs.	MV	3.02	123
and whither fly the gnats but to the sun?	H6c	2.06	9
is the sun dimm'd, that gnats do fly in it?	TIT	4.04	82
till the flies and gnats of nile | have bursed	ANT	3.13	166
and princes not doing so are like to gnats.	PER	2.03	62
gnats are unnoted wheresoe'er they fly. | but	LUC		1014
GNAW 7 FR 0.0006 REL FR	FR	7 V	0 P
wolves are gnarling who shall gnaw thee first.	2H6	3.01	192
that he could gnaw a crust at two hours old.	R3	2.04	28
take these rats thither | to gnaw their garners.	COR	1.01	250
the canker gnaw thy heart, | for showing me	TIM	4.03	50
doth, like a poisonous mineral, gnaw my inwards.	OTH	2.01	297
and hell gnaw his bones!		4.02	136
alas, why gnaw you so your nether lip?		5.02	43
GNAW'D 2 FR 0.0002 REL FR		2 V	0 P
but he, i thank him, gnaw'd in two my cords.	ERR	5.01	290
a thousand men that fishes gnaw'd upon:	R3	1.04	25
GNAWING 3 FR 0.0003 REL FR		3 V	0 P
till, gnawing with my teeth my bonds in sunder.	ERR	5.01	250
thy other hand | gnawing with thy teeth, and he	TIT	3.01	261
to ease the gnawing vulture of thy mind. | by		5.02	31
GNAWN 1 FR 0.0001 REL FR		0 V	1 P
my coffers ransack'd. my reputation gnawn at.	WIV	2.02	293 P
GNAWS 2 FR 0.0002 REL FR		2 V	0 P
that gnaws the bowels of the commonwealth.	1H6	3.01	73
the king is angry. see. he gnaws his lip.	R3	4.02	27
/GO 10 FR 0.0011 REL FR	FR 1293 V	9 V	1 P
/go /some /of /you. /and /fetch /a	R2	4.01	268
/then /give /me /leave /to /go.		4.01	313
/go /some /of /you. /convey /him /to /the /tower		4.01	316
/yet /did /you /say. '/go /forth!'	2H4	1.01	175
/lavinia, /go /with /me	TIT	3.02	81
/and /go /read /with /thee | /sad /stories		3.02	82
/boy, /and /go /with /me. /thy /sight /is /young		3.02	84
/go /thou.	LR	3.07	106
/i /pray /you /go | /along /with /me.		4.03	54
/go /to. /farewell.	OTH	1.03	380 P
GO 1786 FR 0.2018 FR 1293 V 493 P	TMP		
go make thyself like a nymph o' th' sea:		1.02	301
go take this shape | and hither come in't.		1.02	303
go.		1.02	304
we would so. and then go a–batfowling.		1.02	185 P
go sleep. and hear us.		2.01	190 P
so. king. go safely on to seek thy son		2.01	327
with a tang. | would cry to a sailor. 'go hang!'		2.02	51

Fig. 1. (a) Verbal index: L. Hancock's *Word Index to James Joyce's Portrait of the Artist* (1967); (b) Lexicon: A. Schmidt's *Shakespeare Lexicon* (1874); (c) Concordance: M. Spevack's *Harvard Concordance to Shakespeare* (1973). The illustrations are rearranged to show the characteristics of the different forms.

department has changed computers and is about to change to another. Rather than add to an increasingly obsolescent literature, I will restrict my comments here to six areas of consideration of fundamental concern to the concordancer: (1) the selection of the base text; (2) the arrangement of the concordance; (3) the organization of entries; (4) comprehensiveness; (5) the provision of statistical aids; and (6) additional editorial matter. Some further mention will be made of (7) special kinds of concordances.

CHAPTER 2

SELECTION OF BASE TEXT

NOT a few concordances have been compromised from their very inception by the injudicious selection of a text on which the concordance is to be based. The base text is not only the source of the entries in the concordance as it is eventually published, it is the authority for what the concordance contains and the ultimate recourse of the concordance user for information not to be found in the concordance: the base text is *ontos* and *telos*, alpha and omega, the beginning and end of the common concern of the concordancer and the reader. The editor takes the text as content and gives it another form in the concordance; the user studies the rearranged material and returns finally to the original literary text. Consequently the selection of the base text is of paramount importance. In his choice the concordancer is guided by the following considerations.

Authority

In the best of all possible worlds the concordancer has available to him an edition of the kind defined by Professor F. T. Bowers in these words:

"A text may be called 'definitive': or 'established' (a) when an editor has exhaustively determined the authority, in whole and in part, of all preserved documents containing the work under examination; (b) when the text is then based on the most authoritative documents produced in the work's publishing history; and (c) when the complete textual data of all appropriate documents is recorded, together with a full account of all divergences from the edition chosen as copy-text (the basis for the edited text) so that the student may recover the meaningful (substantive) readings of any document used in the preparation of the edited text."[4]

Examples of such an edition are Bowers's own editions of Dekker (1953—61), Marlowe (1973), and Beaumont and Fletcher (1966— in progress), or the CEAA edition of the poems of Stephen Crane edited by Professor M. J. Bruccoli, and Professor J. Katz's *The Poems of Stephen Crane* (New York, Cooper Square, 1966, 2nd rev. printing, 1972): each of the Crane editions, perhaps not surprisingly, is concorded.[5] More often the prospective concordance editor does not have to choose between editions of comparable merit but has, instead, to deal with a number of editions of different age, inclusiveness, accessibility, and price.[6]

The authority of the edition selected as the base text for a concordance depends on how nearly it fits such a definition as that given. However, as I remarked elsewhere, "the scholarly authority of a concordance depends primarily on the authority of the texts selected for concording".[7] This is why one must stress — at the risk of tedious repetition — that the selection of the base text is crucial to the success of the concordance. A concordance to an inferior text invites supercession regardless of the skill of the concordancer in presenting it to the public in concordance form. In words printed elsewhere, "a concordance cannot achieve correctness and textual authority superior to those of the texts of which it is a re-arrangement".[8]

Comprehensiveness

A standard or definitive edition will usually contain the whole canon of the author's works or a coherent part of it, the complete plays, or the like. An edition which presents only a selection of the author's works will not usually commend itself as a base text because the concordance editor would be obliged to complete the canon from other sources in order to present the fullest possible array of linguistic data in the concordance. Since the orthographical details of a second base text are not likely to be consistent with those of the first, the concordancer would find that difficulties of pre-editing, data preparation, and concordance arrangement were appreciably increased, whereas the user of the concordance would not be aided by being obliged to refer to Professor X's edition for some works, Professor Y's selection for other works, and to a selection of manuscripts in libraries thousands of miles away for other details.

Accessibility

In short the base text (or texts) for a concordance must be accessible. The edition should be one likely to be available in most libraries and preferably in print — or likely to be maintained in print — so individual scholars could purchase a copy for private use with the concordance in their studies. There would be little point, for example, in basing a concordance to the writings of Aubrey Beardsley — which no doubt will be a deficiency repaired in time — on a limited edition published in elephant folio format and lavishly illustrated with Beardsley's erotic drawings, which was preserved for the instruction and delectation of mature readers only in the "Treasure Rooms" of a few large libraries. The concordance editor should not neglect to consider that if his author is relatively obscure, his works may not be re-edited for many years, and a fresh concordance may never be called for. A published concordance is portable: it will not be superseded by computer networks, remote access terminals or data storage, and display devices conceivably available to the general public in the next millennium. The concordance editor should devise his concordance for posterity.

Cheapness

When other considerations are equal, as they rarely are, a cheap edition should be preferred to a more costly one as a base text. Professor P. J. Korshin, for example, noted in relation to Michael Shinagel's *A Concordance to the Poems of Jonathan Swift* (Ithaca, NY, Cornell Univ. Press, (1972) which was based on the three-volume second edition by Sir Harold Williams (Oxford, Clarendon Press, 1958) that Herbert Davis's one-volume *Poetical Works* (1967) differed only slightly and was more readily available; he further observed:

"When we are confronted as with Swift, with two nearly identical possibilities, I would think that the shorter, less expensive text would be preferable ... the choice of text has much to do with the concordance's usability".[9]

In all matters other than the authority of the base text, which is paramount, the convenience of the user must rule.

Copyright

It is a matter of practical wisdom as well as law and courtesy for the prospective concordance editor to seek permission of the publishers of his intended base text to prepare a concordance to it. Publication of a concordance helps to confer status on the edition on which it was based and stimulates sales of the edition. Usually publishers are not loath to allow concordancers to use their editions, as I found when I advised the Clarendon Press on such proposals in the 1960s. Moreover, the concordancer who applies to the publishers may learn that permission to concord has already been granted and so save himself much labour (if publication is the main intention) or, usefully, that a revised edition is underway, to incorporate the variants of which would greatly enhance the value of a concordance. There are advantages in being authorized as well as authoritative, particularly if the publisher of the base text becomes interested in publishing the concordance.

Absence of Standard Text

When there is no comprehensive edition prepared according to sound modern principles and generally accepted as "standard", the would-be concordancer has problems. In such an event it sometimes occurs that much of the impetus for a concordance derives from dissatisfaction with existing editions. Work may already be in progress towards a definitive edition for which a concordance would supply an invaluable working tool. A concordance made to an edition in the course of preparation would necessarily be provisional since the materials to render it authoritative — a definitive edition — would not exist and it would be based on existing defective texts. However, parts of the concordance could be updated progressively to provide an increasingly reliable index to the evidence drawn upon by textual editors.[10] Ordinarily such a concordance would not be published before the edition on which it was based.

However, if there were no existing plans for a definitive edition but a widely felt need for a concordance — as is the case with Ben Jonson's dramatic works which I intend to concord myself — there is good cause to publish a concordance which has as its source texts those textual materials which might go towards the preparation of a definitive edition.[11] That course would be practical in normal circumstances only if the author were major and his works required a fair amount of editorial consideration before a definitive edition became possible. The Oxford Shakespeare concordances to the best early old-spelling editions (the good quartos and First Folio texts) are an example of what I have called a "textual concordance" — being concordances to particular states of the author's text — in distinction to the "canonical concordance" which presents a complete concordance to a standard or definitive edition of the author's works. The *Harvard Shakespeare Concordance*, edited by Professor Marvin Spevack, is a prime example of the "canonical concordance": it is based on *The Riverside Shakespeare* (Houghton Mifflin, 1974) edited by Professor G.B. Evans.

A concordance of somewhat different kind in respect of base text although similar to the *Oxford Shakespeare Concordance* as a "textual concordance" is the Ingram-Swaim Milton concordance. It comes close to being a "variorum concordance", for it approaches definitiveness and comprehensiveness by supplying records of significant readings from multiple manuscript sources: it is substantially based "on the texts of Milton's poems that were published in his lifetime, on certain authoritative manuscripts of the same period, and in a few instances on later seventeenth century texts as well. It is not based on any modern edition of the poems.[12]

Such "textual concordances", in Professor Ingram's words, "serve as an index to the editor's evidence and not to his conclusions". They can be justified when, for older authors, facsimiles of the early texts are available or, for modern authors, the texts themselves are widely available in research libraries. Their main disadvantage is that there is not a single source to which the user can refer when pursuing his studies beyond the confines of the concordance: that is the price paid for the benefit of comprehensiveness.

Pre-editing

Once the concordance editor has selected the base text, he will represent it in machine-readable and, ultimately, published form with a degree of fidelity which is determined by the purposes to which the concordance will be put. There is no point, for example, in retaining ligatures like ĉt which would not be studied — if they were to be studied at all — directly from a concordance. Special characters, which do not affect the sort order (like diaereses and long s) but are difficult to retain in the computer and print, may be silently omitted with a note to that effect in the introduction to the concordance. Indeed, the specific occurrences of such immaterial signs like the occasional circumflexes in Shakespeare's early texts could be listed in the introduction to avoid their retention in the concordance at great cost of programming and effort but to little perceptible benefit. The considerations which apply to these peripheral matters are specific to the author and to the computing and publishing facilities available to the concordancer and need not be discussed in detail here. In general, however, the concordance will retain the substantives and significant accidentals of the base texts. Amongst "significant accidentals" should be included capitalization and italicization which are especially important for the older authors and convey a wealth of information to the perceptive reader.

On the other hand, the concordance editor must resist the temptation to embellish or tamper with his text. When the concordancer does not have a standard base text available to him, or does not intend to produce a "textual concordance" to the materials for a definitive edition, it doubtless takes nerve to publish a concordance to an avowedly deficient edition. Yet, if it is to be done at all, that is what the concordance editor must steel himself to do. The grounds for this stringent attitude are these. The establishment of a definitive text and the preparation of a base text for concording are distinct tasks, dependent on expertise and abilities not commonly found in a single editor. Professor David Erdman's Cornell Blake concordance is the exception which proves the rule.[13] If the concordance rather than the edition is the editor's goal, textual analysis will probably be hasty and imperfect: a superficial consistency for the aid of computation will be imported into texts of various origins for the editing of which significantly different principles should apply. Mere tinkering, a less than thorough-going recension and establishment of the text, would subject the concordance to crushing criticism *qua* text. Furthermore, such a text used as the source of a concordance, as I have already remarked, would not supply a public base text for the user of the concordance when an extended context for the occurrence of a particular form was necessary.

It may be desirable for a concordance editor to import into a published standard base-text corrections which were themselves published, but he would not do this without notice to the user, both in the introduction and in the concordance contexts by the use of sigla to indicate a departure from the base text. Nothing is so quickly destructive of confidence in a concordance than a user's discovery that the text of the concordance and the base text differ in substantive readings.

CHAPTER 3

ARRANGEMENT

Alphabetization

The most common arrangement of the heading words in a concordance is alphabetical.[14] Arrangement in the order of the English alphabet seems preferable since English-speakers learn the order at an early age and, since the order has remained static in English (apart from *i/j* and *u/v*) for hundreds of years, concordances so arranged are the most generally and most readily accessible. Nevertheless, there are problems in connection with characters other than the basic A to Z.

Numerals like Falstaff's "iiii.d" for "Sawce" (*1H4* 2.4.536) are best sorted with the verbal form, e.g. FOUR, when the number nouns or adjectives of order ("first, second,") occur in the text already. When they do not, and for dates like "1826", it is better to leave them where they occur according to the common computer sort, either before or after the A-Z sequence, and to provide references to the number form from the appropriate alphabetical position. Ampersands (&) and "&c." also should be sorted with AND and ETC. or ETCETERA where those entries occur in the main sequence. The same principles hold with other parallel forms and contractions like "L." for "Lord" and "St." for "saint". The best procedure in this and other aspects of concording is to consult the convenience of the user and list shortened forms with the full forms when they exist, and to provide references when they do not.

Hyphenated Compounds

Foremost amongst the trouble-making characters a concordance editor must deal with are hyphens: these are associated with two distinct areas of difficulty. The first is authorial inconsistency, which from text to text produces a melange of forms like HOME MADE, HOME-MADE, and HOMEMADE; publishers' house style may be responsible for some of such inconsistency. The concordancer may wish all forms to be noticed under the first component HOME or seek to have the compounds listed together. This is more easily decided than achieved, for the hyphen has a specific value in sorting which affects the order of words containing them: this is the second area of difficulty. In some computer character sets the hyphen sorts before A-Z, in others, after A-Z.[15] In order to adhere to strict alphabetization it is necessary for a hyphenated form like A-SLEEP to be listed before or after ASLEEP where the user would expect to find it. Concordance editors have adopted various expedients to deal with the hyphen. None of the five is entirely satisfactory: the concordancer's choice must be determined by the nature and extent of hyphenation and compounding in the basic text.

Hyphen as Space

For the Cornell Arnold concordance the programme assigned hyphens the sort value of the space, thus converting the text's GREEN-MUFFLED, for instance, into two separately listed words.[16] But the compound itself was lost as a HW. (The Cornell programme was subsequently revised to retain the hyphens.)

Hyphen Suppression

In computer programmes which create a sort key — a sequence of characters which determines the order of the sorted items but not necessarily the style of the printed HW — the hyphen can be suppressed, that is, omitted entirely, so that entries containing A-SLEEP and HOME-MADE would be sorted with entries for the non-hyphenated form. However, in programmes in which the sort key and the HW are essentially the same, hyphen suppression would produce HWs like GENERALPURPOSE and NOTTOBEACCEPTED.

Dummy Hyphens

Another expedient is to insert rather than suppress hyphens in non-hyphenated compounds. Hence, in the Cornell Blake concordance, the HW CORN-FIELD, CORN FIELD stands before the entries for both hyphenated and unhyphenated forms listed together.[17] Insertion, however, unlike suppression which may be automatic, must be an editorial function.

Hyphen Less than A-Z

Considerable dislocation of the expected alphabetical order will occur if the hyphen takes a value less than A-Z during the sort, or a greater value.

Hyphen Greater than A-Z

According to the value of the hyphen entries will sort automatically into one of the following illustrative sequences.

A	A
A-SLEEP	AARDVARK
A-YAWN	ABLE
AARDVARK	ASLEEP
ABLE	AYAWN
ASLEEP	A-SLEEP
AYAWN	A-YAWN
HOME	HOME
HOME-MADE	HOMELY
HOMELY	HOMEMADE
HOMEMADE	HOMES
HOMES	HOME-MADE
HUB	HUB

Many concordance programmes provide facilities for rearrangement of entries after the first indexing and sort; where they do not it is not difficult to write a simple programme to provide for re-sorting. Many concordance editors are prepared to accept one of the orders above but should never do so silently: the consequences for the user should always be spelled out specifically in the introduction to the published concordance — which a user ignores at his peril.

The consistent treatment of simple compounds like HOMEMADE and hyphenated compounds concerns the concordance editor. The best practice seems to be to enter the compound in the form in which it occurs, with references amongst the parts as necessary, except when, as in the Cornell Blake concordance and the Oxford Shakespeare concordances, subsequent parts of hyphenated compounds are separately entered under the appropriate HWs.[18]

Old and Modern Spelling Heading Words

There are sufficient differences between English and American spellings of certain kinds of words (e.g. *-ise/ize, -er/re*) to oblige the concordance editor to consider what provision he should make for variant spellings. In a concordance to the works of an English author the preferable procedure is to refer from the usual English spelling of the HW to any other spelling which may be present; for American authors the American spelling is standard. Many authors of the nineteenth century are represented by works first published on either side of the Atlantic and orthographic variation may be so extensive as to suggest to the concordancer the desirability of listing all occurrences of a word under a single HW regardless of the spelling of the various instances. That is reasonable practice for more modern authors if orthography itself is not likely to be one aspect of the works which a user might expect to study with the aid of the concordance, or if the subsumption of lines containing variant spellings under a single heading is not attended by ambiguity. For older authors — at least to the end of the seventeenth century — variant spellings afford the concordancer many complex problems which are difficult to resolve correctly.

A concordance to an author like Spenser or Shakespeare will reveal a variety of spellings which may reflect not only the number of scribes and compositors who might have had a hand in the transmission of the text, or the author's own indifference to an established consistent orthography, but also the flux of the language itself. The editor of the concordance has two options: (i) to retain the HW in the original spelling. This is commendable for its simplicity and ease but the editor will be obliged to supply numerous references from the modern form of the HW — or, more often, the old spelling HW like OLDE found where the user would expect to find the modern spelling — to all variant spelling HWs listed in the concordance. If he does not refer to *all* variant forms he will be chided by reviewers (as I know from my own experience) for not referring to a variant which follows the entry for the main form but does not occur on the same page, a deficiency which sometimes is not apparent until the final stages in preparation of the concordance. A sound practice, it seems, and one which I have adopted in an unpublished concordance to the Shakespeare First Folio, is to list after the main HW (that is, the HW most like the modern form which occurs in the sequence of the alphabet where the modern user would expect it) all spelling variants occurring in the concordance. Hypothetical examples are SHERIFF (SHERIF, SHERIFE, SHREEUE, SHREIUE, SHREUE, SHRIEUE) or AGAINST (AGENST) *see also* 'GAINST. The second example shows the addition of reference to the apheretic form of "against" which should not, to anticipate the argument at this point, be considered simply as a spelling variant.[19]

(ii) The second option is to list occurrences of variant spellings under the modern spelling of the word, the method of the Ingram-Swaim Milton concordance (Fig. 2), to mention but one example. This procedure gives two benefits: users whose concern is principally with the word and not with the various orthographies in which it might appear, will locate the correct HW and entries with little difficulty, and, even more usefully, the entries under the HW, although they contain different spellings of the HW form, will be in serial order of the base text — this, too, facilitates reference. The main objection to the practice is that the burden of sorting the material under the HW is shifted back from the computer to the user. There is an exquisite irony in the fact that the computer will have sorted the entries for a text into order of the old spellings in it, the concordance editor will have amalgamated entries with different spellings under a single HW, and the user who seeks spellings of a particular kind, or a single instance of an uncommon spelling, must sort them out again. For a large corpus secondary sorting by the user may be more onerous than might be thought. In the Shakespeare First Folio, for example,

Daisies
The Wood-Nymphs deckt with Daisies trim,   Mask 120
  Trinity ms 'daysies'
  1637 'daisies'
  Bridgewater ms 'daisies'
Meadows trim with Daisies pide,   Allegro 75

Dale
The flowry Dale of *Sibma* clad with Vines,   Par Lost 1.410
  ms 'dale'
With winged course ore Hill or moarie Dale,   Par Lost 2.944
Powrd forth profuse on Hill and Dale and Plaine,   Par Lost 4.243
Through wood, through waste, o're hill, o're dale his roam.   Par Lost 4.538
Of pleasure situate in Hill and Dale)   Par Lost 6.641
Hill, Dale, and shadie Woods, and sunnie Plaines,   Par Lost 8.262
Well have we speeded, and o're hill and dale,   Par Reg 3.267
And sweeten'd every muskrose of the dale,   Mask 496
  Trinity ms 'dale' ←'valley'
Under the Hawthorn in the dale.   Allegro 68
From haunted spring, and dale   Nativity 184
Hill and Dale, doth boast thy blessing.   May Morn 8
As through a fruitfull watry Dale   Psalm 84, 23

Dales
Ye Hills and Dales, ye Rivers, Woods, and Plaines,   Par Lost 8.275
O Woods, O Fountains, Hillocks, Dales and Bowrs,   Par Lost 10.860
Of *Caucasus*, and dark *Iberian* dales,   Par Reg 3.318

Dalila
Was in the Vale of *Sorec*, *Dalila*,   Samson 229
Then *Dalila* thy wife.   Samson 724
The sumptuous *Dalila* floating this way: Samson 1072
Of *Philistean Dalilah*, and wak'd   Par Lost 9.1061

Dalliance
Of dalliance had with thee in Heav'n, and joys   Par Lost 2.819
Wanted, nor youthful dalliance as beseems   Par Lost 4.338
Held dalliance with his faire *Egyptian* Spouse.   Par Lost 9.443
Till *Adam* thus 'gan *Eve* to dalliance move,   Par Lost 9.1016

Dally
Let our frail thoughts dally with false surmise.   Lycidas 153

Dam
Slip't from the fold, or young Kid lost his dam,   Mask 498
  Trinity ms 'damme'

Damage
My damage fondly deem'd, I can repaire   Par Lost 7.152

Damasco
Damasco, or *Marocco*, or *Trebisond*,   Par Lost 1.584
  ms 'Damasco'

Damascus
Was fair *Damascus*, on the fertil Banks   Par Lost 1.468
  ms 'Damascus'
Damasco, or *Marocco*, or *Trebisond*,   Par Lost 1.584
  ms 'Damasco'

Damaskd
On the soft downie Bank damaskt with flours: Par Lost 4.334

Dame
Sovran of Creatures, universal Dame.   Par Lost 9.612
Of mid-night Torches burns; mysterious Dame   Mask 130
  Bridgewater ms 'dame'

Dames
Count the night watches to his feathery Dames,   Mask 347
  Trinity ms 'dames'
  Bridgewater ms 'dames'
Stoutly struts his Dames before,   Allegro 52

Damiata
Betwixt *Damiata* and mount *Casius* old,   Par Lost 2.593

Damietta
Betwixt *Damiata* and mount *Casius* old,   Par Lost 2.593

Dammd
Or if your influence be quite damm'd up   Mask 336
  Trinity ms 'dam'd'

Damnation
Heap on himself damnation, while he sought   Par Lost 1.215

Damned
His own: for neither do the Spirits damn'd   Par Lost 2.482
O shame to men! Devil with Devil damn'd   Par Lost 2.496
At certain revolutions all the damn'd   Par Lost 2.597
To do what else though damnd I should abhorre.   Par Lost 4.392
That Evil one, Satan for ever damn'd.   Par Reg 4.194
Where that damn'd wizard hid in sly disguise   Mask 571
  1637 'dam'd'
But for that damn'd magician, let him be girt   Mask 602
Can in his swadling bands controul the damned crew.   Nativity 228

Damoetas
And old *Damoetas* luv'd to hear our song.   Lycidas 36

Dampe
  Bridgewater ms 'dampe'

Damps
Accompanied, with damps and dreadful gloom,   Par Lost 10.848
From dews and damps of night his shelter'd head,   Par Reg 4.406

Damsel
Her harbinger, a damsel train behind;   Samson 721
And put the Damsel to suspicious flight,   Mask 158
  Trinity ms 'damsel'
  Bridgewater ms 'damsell'
She guiltless damsell flying the mad pursuit   Mask 829
  1673 'damsel'
By boistrous rape th' Athenian damsel got,   Fair Inf 9

Damsels
The *Syrian* Damsels to lament his fate   Par Lost 1.448
  ms 'damsells'
Of Fairy Damsels met in Forest wide   Par Reg 2.359

Dan
Doubl'd that sin in *Bethel* and in *Dan*,   Par Lost 1.485
  ms 'Dan'
Of *Bethel* and of *Dan?* no, let them serve   Par Reg 3.431
Man. Brethren and men of *Dan*, for such ye seem,   Samson 332
In *Dan*, in *Judah*, and the bordering Tribes,   Samson 976
In the camp of *Dan*   Samson 1436

Danaw
Rhene or the *Danaw*, when her barbarous Sons   Par Lost 1.353
  ms 'Danaw'

Dance
Wheels her pale course, they on thir mirth and dance   Par Lost 1.786
  ms defective here
Lur'd with the smell of infant blood, to dance   Par Lost 2.664
Thir Starry dance in numbers that compute   Par Lost 3.580
Knit with the *Graces* and the *Hours* in dance   Par Lost 4.267
Mixt Dance, or wanton Mask, or Midnight Bal,   Par Lost 4.768
In mystic Dance not without Song, resound   Par Lost 5.178
In song and dance about the sacred Hill,   Par Lost 5.619
Mystical dance, which yonder starrie Sphear   Par Lost 5.620
Forthwith from dance to sweet repast they turn   Par Lost 5.630
As they would dance, yet for a dance they seemd   Par Lost 5.615
Rose as in Dance the stately Trees, and spred   Par Lost 7.324
Incited, dance about him various rounds?   Par Lost 8.125
Noise, other then the sound of Dance or Song,   Par Lost 8.243
Soft amorous Ditties, and in dance came on: Par Lost 11.584
Of lustful appetence, to sing, to dance,   Par Lost 11.619
To luxurie and riot, feast and dance,   Par Lost 11.715
Tipsie dance, and Jollity.   Mask 104
  Bridgewater ms 'daunce'
In wanton dance they praise the bounteous *Pan*,   Mask 176
  Bridgewater ms 'daunce'
By all the *Nymphs* that nightly dance   Mask 883
  Bridgewater ms 'daunce'
With Jiggs, and rural dance resort,   Mask 952
  Bridgewater ms 'daunce'
To triumph in victorious dance   Mask 974
  B.M. ms 'Daunce'
  Bridgewater ms 'Daunce'
Nymphs and Shepherds dance no more   Arcades 96
In dismall dance about the furnace blue,   Nativity 210
Both they who sing, and they who dance   Psalm 87, 25

Danced
Danc'd hand in hand. A while discourse they hold;   Par Lost 5.395
Dawn, and the *Pleiades* before him danc'd   Par Lost 7.374
Terrestrial Heav'n, danc't round by other Heav'ns   Par Lost 9.103
Rough *Satyrs* danc'd, and *Fauns* with clov'n heel,   Lycidas 34
  Trinity ms 'danc't'
The Faiery Ladies daunc't upon the hearth;   Vacation 60

Dancers
Juglers and Dancers, Antics, Mummers, Mimics,   Samson 1325

Dances
That flames, and dances in his crystal bounds   Mask 673

Dancing
Thou couldst repress, nor did the dancing Rubie   Samson 543
Dancing in the Chequer'd shade;   Allegro 96
Comes dancing from the East, and leads with her   May Morn 2

Dandl'd
Dandl'd the Kid; Bears, Tygers, Ounces, Pards,   Par Lost 4.344

Danger
If counsels different, or danger shun'd   Par Lost 1.636
Pondering the danger with deep thoughts; and each   Par Lost 2.421
Of difficulty or danger could deterr   Par Lost 2.449
So much the neerer danger; go and speed;   Par Lost 2.1008
Which else might work him danger or delay: Par Lost 3.635

Fig. 2. Ingram-Swaim Milton concordance, p. 110. Variant spellings are subsumed under single modern-spelling heading words.

there are 4549 entries which could be listed under the modern-spelling HW WILL; it would not be easy for a user interested in the effect of justification on spelling to locate the 124 occurrences of "wil" amongst such a large number of entries.

In order to render an old-spelling concordance useful to as many potential users possible, the concordance editor would feel obliged, if he did not list the spelling variants after the HW (as in the SHERIFF example above), to insert references in the positions which would have been occupied by variant-spelling HWs to the modern-spelling HW under which the variants were listed. Hence, to use SHERIFF as an example, there would need to be six references (one for each variant) of the form SHREEUE *see* SHERIFF. On the other hand, had the HWs been left in their first sorted order only one reference (SHERIFF *see also* SHERIF, SHERIFE, SHREEUE, SHERIUE, SHREUE, SHRIEUE) would be necessary once the practice was established that variant spellings were displayed at the point where the modern-spelling HW should be expected to occur. There is a danger, apart from other awkwardnesses of use if the modern-spelling HW option is adopted, that a concordance to a corpus with considerable spelling variation may appear to consist mainly of cross-references.[20]

Treatment of i/j and u/v

The concordance editor who retains old-spelling HWs will not ordinarily normalise *i/j* as in *ioy, iniurious* and *u/v* as in *vs, aduise* in the base text. Even in texts which have modern editions there may be inconsistencies in the use of these characters which would result in multiple HWs if special measures are not devised to deal with the problem. There is no advantage, for example, in recording *pervse* for *peruse* in the Folio *Merchant of Venice* (line 831) or *serv'd* for *seru'd* in *The Tempest* (line 372) under separate HWs. Inconsistencies may be removed if the computer is programmed to treat all *j*'s as *i*'s and all *v*'s as *u*'s for sorting purposes and in HWs. Nevertheless, the resultant order of HWs may be unfamiliar to some users, to their detriment when, for example, ADUISED is listed before ADULTERY. I do not regard this as too great an impediment to old-spelling HWs to be

removed by the judicious provisions of references, and the phenom-
enon is mentioned simply so the careful concordance editor can take
account of it.

Homograph Distinction

Professor Demetrius Koubourlis uses the expression *homoform
insensitivity* to refer to "the lumping together of homographic forms
on the basis of spelling identity alone without taking phonological
and semantic differences into account".[21] The computer, as everyone
knows, sorts on the basis of a predetermined order of characters,
usually the English alphabet, and therefore entries which contain the
same sequence of characters are listed under a single HW without
distinction. Hence the HW GODS may be followed by entries which
contain instances of (1) the nominative plural (*gods*), (2) the genitive
singular (*god's*), (3) the genitive plural (*gods'*) and (4) the noun-verb
elision (*god's* = god is). Although a sorting procedure sensitive to
apostrophes would distinguish (1), (2), and (3), the second category
would still contain (4), and if the base text was inconsistent in the use
of apostrophes — as early modern printed texts and manuscripts
usually are — or did not use apostrophes at all — like Old and Middle
English texts — not even that degree of distinction could be achieved
automatically by a programme which used formal discriminants. In
practice, a sort which took account of apostrophes might increase
"homoform insensitivity": special procedures would be necessary to
cope with expressions like "'Happy is the man favoured by the gods'"
where the terminal single quotation mark would sort a nominative
plural as a genitive plural, or "spare me your constant 'By God's'",
where the original nominative singular is plural in the reported speech
but would be treated as a genitive singular by a programme which
used the apostrophe in the sort.

As the example of GODS goes some way towards showing, the task
of distinguishing amongst homographs is not a light one, particularly
when lexically distinct forms are obscured in old-spelling texts by
spelling variation. The crucial question for a concordance editor who
contemplates homograph distinction is to decide how far to pursue it,
for, adopted whole heartedly, homograph distinction leads finally to

a dictionary arrangement. Four general kinds of distinction are possible. (1) Simplest to distinguish are *orthographic homographs*, "words" which are orthographically different (*do, doe, doo*) but the same morpheme, being different spellings of one morpheme (*do*). (2) *Graphemic homographs* are forms which are graphemically different (*god, god's, god'[i]s*) — when the language has a highly developed orthography — but are morphemically similar, being different graphemes of the two morphemes of the word *god*. (3) *Homonymic homographs* are words which are graphemically similar (*art/lead/will* as both nouns and verbs) but morphemically dissimilar: they agree in spelling but are different in origin and meaning. (4) Finally, there are *polysemantic homographs* which are words like *act* which have several meanings.[22]

If a concordance editor decides to list orthographic homographs, (1), under a single HW, he will inevitably be led into more thorough-going homograph distinction because he will have to determine which form to list variant spellings under. If he is at all interested in providing statistics he must amalgamate spellings under HWs so the count of "words" is not inflated by spelling variation. Further consideration of statistical rigour — not to mention linguistic propriety — will enforce steps (2) and (3) on him. The arrangement of HWs is shortened by the first step and is inflated by the third. Distinction of polysemantic homographs, (4), should not be considered, for reasons which are touched on in the next chapter and again under "lemmatization". The object of the distinction should be to ensure that forms which the "common reader" perceives as distinct would not be grouped together: I mention "common reader" because it is unwise to assume that only linguists will use a concordance. Hence the common user who is made uncomfortable by a mixture of the noun and verb *will* under a single HW, and the conglomeration under GODS, will acknowledge the propriety of recording the genitive singular and verb elision under the HW GOD, and the genitive plural under the nominative plural GODS, and of separating instances of homonyms. I do not believe distinction in the concordance arrangement should extend so far as conjugations and inflexions: that seems a lexicographical function.

Even to achieve homographic distinction on this fairly basic level is beyond the capacity of computers to accomplish without the aid of pre- or post-editing. A forceful argument against pre-editing is that the complete range of lexical forms is not known to the concordance editor in advance: he requires a concordance in order to mark up text for a concordance. There appears no practical alternative than to post-edit the raw-concorded data.[23] Post-editing is complicated and time consuming, particularly when the corpus is linguistically complex and lexical aids are inadequate. Every entry under every HW susceptible to homonymy — which means virtually every monosyllabic form and up to half the rest — must be examined and assigned a discriminator for a second sort. The concordance editor will encounter many specific problems, such as elisions — if *god's* is to be sorted under GOD, should not *I'll* be entered under I; but what should be done about the verbal complements, *'s* and *'ll*?

Ambiguity

The most difficult problems of lexical taxonomy reside in the ambiguity inherent in literary English, and especially in the older forms of the tongue. Puns, malapropisms, and other forms of word-play do not fit comfortably in lexical schemes; indeed, sometimes it is difficult to decide whether or not a pun exists. At different periods distinct meanings will come to have distinctive orthographies (e.g. *human/humane*; *travel/travail*), the distinctive spelling having already existed or having been specially created in order to distinguish senses. (It is a chastening reflection that students need to be told that originally *human* was *humane*.) But whether one or other of the possible senses is denoted by the variant spelling may not be possible for the concordance editor to determine in an individual case without extensive linguistic investigation which it is not his function to undertake. Very often such ambiguities are not resolved by modern editors who avail themselves of the freedom provided by footnotes to comment "Perhaps a pun is intended" or "Possibly to be interpreted as ...", and similar expressions. On other occasions texts may create the concordance editor's problems rather than merely fail to resolve them. Textual cruxes which lack generally agreeable solutions may lead users to expect information from a concordance which is not to be found there, and sometimes to impute error to the concordancer.

The scholar seeks in vain in the Harvard *Concordance to Shakespeare* for Hamlet's "too too solid flesh" at 1.2.129 for "solid" is the reading of the First Folio text which was not adopted by the New Riverside editor. Moreover, if he looks under *sullied*, which is often taken as the modern spelling of the reading of the good second quarto, he will find nothing but a reference to SALLIED, the original reading. The popular expression, "a rose by any other name" also is missing, the editor correctly having preferred the "word" of the good quarto of *Romeo and Juliet*. A crux at *Hamlet* 2.2.182 may be resolved as "a god kissing carrion", where carrion is "dead putrefying flesh", or as "a good kissing carrion" where the use of carrion is figurative and carnal. On a grammatical level of homographic distinction the ambiguity creates no difficulty, but if distinction is pursued at the semantic level, the concordancer may face insurmountable problems.

As a practical question I believe the concordance editor should attempt to distinguish homographs on the grammatical level, to an extent determined by the complexity of the base text — when the base text is not a standard or definitive text he would find it hard to go very far — and by the degree to which he can assume the user will follow him. If the distinctions he must make involve analysis and considerations which draw on material lying outside the scope of the concordance, he should desist, since the user will not have access to the same material. The concordance editor must always explain in the introduction to the concordance the course he has chosen and the grounds for its adoption.[24]

Lemmatization

To go beyond the simplest form of homograph distinction leads the concordance editor to the dictionary, the scope of which is far greater than that of the concordance. To assert that concordances should be lexicons, as Dr. Koubourlis appears to suggest in the paper already mentioned, comes close to confining to a single area of scholarly concern two distinct kinds of intellectual activity which are embodied in forms only superficially identical. Although the concordance arrangement of lexical items may be extended towards a dictionary arrangement — and possibly should be for highly inflected languages like Russian from which Dr. Koubourlis draws his arguments — lexicons provide only one of several possible arrangements towards which a concordance could grow; these are discussed in a later section. The movement from concordance to dictionary is from the general towards the more specialized and the advantage obtained by more sophisticated arrangements of material may be at the cost of frustrating classes of users who not only may have no use for the information conveyed by the new arrangement but further may be actually inhibited in their use of the concordance by it. It is almost axiomatic that the more complicated the arrangement of a reference tool is, the smaller becomes the number of people who can expect to use it competently.

Concordances precede lexicons; to a great extent they provide the raw data for them. A concordance, as Dr. Ingram has said in other words, gives an index to the data, not to its interpretation; the interpretation is supplied by the individual user with his special perspective and particular inquiry. To advance far along the lexical path is to put the concordance editor, an even duller drudge than the lexicographer, more and more into the realm of interpretation. If the concordance editor attempts to cope with the ambiguities mentioned in the previous section save in a mechanical way, or to distinguish shades of meaning for polysemantic homographs, he usurps a function not naturally his. It is as if, in the textual sphere, no concordance were ever to be made to the works of an inedited author without the concordance editor having first published a definitive edition of the works.

A concordance which scatters the forms of a single word throughout the alphabetical sequence (as with *be/is/was/were, go/gone/went, good/better/best*) instead of listing them under the lemma of the dictionary form is characterized, according to Dr. Koubourlis's useful term, by "word-form diffusion".[25] In a dictionary, one function of which is to show the relationship of one form of a word to another, word-form concentration (i.e. lemmatization) is doubtless desirable, but a concordance which does not pretend to that function achieves little by a lemmatized arrangement. In a concordance characterized by "word-form concentration" often the entries for the different forms are not even on the same opening of pages, so there is no advantage for consultation and comparison, and the concordance editor is obliged to supply references from the naive user's first point of reference — the alphabetical sequence — to the lemmatized location, in the form WENT *see under* GO. That not even the compilers of the *Concordance of Five Middle English Poems*[26] or any other con-cordancer to the present time, whether he used manual or computer methods, have lemmatized entries, is some evidence that arrangement by lemmas for English concordances is not regarded as necessary.

References

The function of cross-references is to repair the integrity of the alphabetical sequence of HWs to compensate for the extent it was weakened by various practices discussed above. The user finds comfort in knowing that all the material indexed by the sequence of HWs is accessible from the point in the sequence at which it was natural for him to commence his inquiry, and the concordance editor should not lightly disappoint him. Even if instances of the occurrence of variant spellings are subsumed under modern-spelling HWs, references from variant spellings to the appropriate HWs should accommodate a user who approaches the concordance on the orthographical or graphemic level. When the order of HWs produced by the first rough sort of the concordance data is changed in any material way, references should direct the user to the rearranged information.

References which are not simply amplifications of existing HWs — such as the labelling of WILL to distinguish the noun and the verb — are of two kinds: *see* references and *see also* references. It continually amazes me that scholars who use dictionary catalogues in their university libraries day after day do not appear to appreciate the distinct functions of the two kinds of references. A *see* reference leads the user from a place in the sequence where there is no information relevant to his inquiry to the place where the information is located. The *see also* reference is attached to a HW already present at the first point of access and refers the reader to *other* information which might assist his inquiry. The direction of reference is usually from the general to the specific, e.g. "IS *see also* all's...", where the user requires to be informed about the verb elisions which occur in a text if IS is his main interest. The reader who looks up ALL does not need to be reminded to consult IS; even if the verb was of interest to him, a reference would be unnecessary to the reader of average intelligence.

The kinds of material for which references should be supplied patently depend on the condition of the language of the works concorded and on the extent of its rearrangement within the common concordance order of HWs. Nevertheless, one can suggest certain categories of material which usually demand references in concordances to English literature: (i) parts of *compounds* and *elisions* not otherwise concorded; (ii) *aphetic* and *apheretic* forms like *'gainst* and *'scape*; (iii) forms normally *compounded*, e.g. *a praying* which will be concorded as an instance of *praying* but requires a reference from A; (iv) *numbers* and contractions like "23, St., &"; (v) *variant spellings*; (vi) any other forms where the order is unexpected, e.g. "ADVISED *see* aduised", "ANGELL *see also* an-gell", in a concordance to the good quarto of *Hamlet*.

CHAPTER 4

ORGANIZATION OF ENTRIES

BENEATH each HW lies a sequence of entries which testifies to the occurrence of the concorded form at different places in the base text. The content of the entries and, to a varying extent, their organization after the heading, are obviously affected by homograph distinction and by the amalgamation of instances of variant spellings, but in the present discussion for the sake of simplicity I intend to disregard any complications or exceptions to general principles which might occur on those accounts.

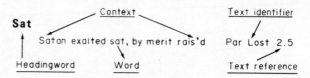

Fig. 3. The fields of a concordance entry.

A single entry consists of four readily identifiable fields, (1) the *context* for occurrence of the particular instance of the form in question, that is, a quotation from the base text in which the concorded word occurs; the context includes (2) the *word* itself, a distinction which becomes significant in relation to KWIC/KWOC concording; (3) the *sigil* which identifies the text which is the source of the context; and (4) the *reference* to the specific line/s or verse/s. In addition some concordances supply (5) a *count* of the number of instances of the concorded word in the entries beneath it, and (6) *other information* about the specific entry (Fig. 3).

Just as the HWs are arranged in the simple but generally accessible A-Z sequence for ease of reference, the separate entries under each

HW should occur in the order which allows quick access to the base text from which the entries were drawn. When the concordance is to a single literary work, like the separate volumes of the *Oxford Shakespeare Concordance,* entries should occur under the HW in *text* order, entries in the first act being followed by entries in acts two to five sequentially. A concordance will usually retain text order even when a number of different works are concorded in a single alphabetical sequence, but in this common case the concordance editor and user alike must attend to the order of reference to separate works in the canon. Many different orders of works are possible. References to individual occurrences of words may be listed according to (i) alphabetical order of titles, e.g. for Shakespeare, *Ado., Ant., AYL, Err... Ven.,* or (ii) publication, or (iii) composition, or (iv) order of appearance in an authoritative collection of the author's works, like the Shakespeare First Folio of 1623: the *Harvard Concordance to Shakespeare* uses this sequence, which runs *Tmp., TGV, ... Cym... Son.*; or (v) order of genres, or (vi) an order in which the titles are classified as works of single authorship, collaborations, and doubtful works. These are the more obvious sequences of citations; it is not difficult to think of others, as, for example, a concordance in which entries for an author's Latin works are listed after those for English work — where, of course, there was a mixture of languages within the canon.

The concordance editor will select the sequence of entries which is likely to be at once both familiar to the users of the concordance and also consistent with the general nature of the corpus and the inquiries likely to be directed to the concordance. (For a discussion of the reason why the alphabetical order of titles is not most frequently chosen, see under (iii) following.) For a Shakespearian concordance, for example, the usefulness of arrangement of entries according to the chronological order of composition is undeniable: it would offer almost at a glance information relevant to a host of pertinent inquiries. Nevertheless, since there is so little agreement about the order of composition of Shakespeare's works, the order chosen by the concordancer for the entries would probably not be that referred to by the user in his own mind when he set about scanning an extensive entry, as many users would be confused by the order as would be helped by it. In another connection it might be suggested that although the Folio order of entries adopted by the Harvard concordance is essential to bibliographers and textual critics seeking information about the habits of compositors and scribes, it is less useful in that concordance where the contexts are modernized and which will be used by a great variety of students to whom "Folio" order is either largely unknown or essentially irrelevant. In any event, the order of entries should be explained and justified in the concordance editor's introduction.[27]

The order of fields in the concordance entry is not random or wilful but designed to afford the easiest access to information. A user with a specific inquiry has in mind at the very least a particular HW: he is accustomed to find headings at the left of a printed page. When he locates the desired HW, if he has a specific text or entry he may find it readily by scanning the sigla and reference field at the right of the entry (and the page). Otherwise, if he does not have an inquiry specific to a text or line, but requires to scan the sequence of entries until he finds the entry or entries which satisfy his inquiry, his eye moves across the page through the context from left to right, towards the reference field, in natural English reading order. The order given above is the most comfortable for readers accustomed to reading from left to right and should not be departed from lightly.

The Context

This is the first item after the HW, wherein the reader seeks to ascertain whether the particular instance of the word is suitable for his purposes. The context may take several different forms as, for example (a) typographical units, a line or lines drawn from the base text. Of course, all contexts are in a sense typographical, being drawn from a printed text, but only when the original orthography is retained and the boundaries of the line indicated — by the conventional end-of-line marker | as in the Oxford Shakespeare Concordances as an aid for a special kind of study — is "typographical" a just description of the context. However, many concordances take a single line of the base text as the unit of entry: so common is this that the imperceptive reader may be forgiven perhaps for mistaking the context as "typographical" and understanding it to be invariable practice. In fact such a context more often than not is (b) a verse of poetry, this metrical unit being the most common of all concordance contexts. There are, furthermore, (c) syntactical contexts such as those determined by computer algorithms from observing the position and frequency of a hierarchy of punctuation marks: this kind of context — of which the most prominent illustration is afforded by the *Harvard Shakespeare Concordance* — deserves closer description in a following part of this book. Then there exists the possibility of two additional kinds of context of which examples are not readily found in the literature, (d) rhetorical units, such as complete speeches of characters in a play, or figures of speech, and (e) semantic units, contexts which include complete segments of meaning rather than a syntactically coherent part like a dependent clause in a sentence.

A fundamental misconception about the essential character of concordances, and hence about the function of contexts, has led to a variety of ill-considered criticisms of them amongst reviewers and users who, from their familiarity with the nature of language and literary expression, should really know better. A published concordance, which necessarily possesses a limited rather than discrete form, is merely an index to literary works and, as an index, does not itself contain all the information necessary to satisfy all the inquiries directed to it. An example will make this point clearer. The index to Herford and Simpson's *Ben Jonson* under "Walley, Henry (publisher)" informs the inquirer that information will be found on page 268 of the seventh volume; it does not reveal that Walley's name is recorded in Arber's *Transcript* in the Stationers' Register entry for Jonson's "The Masque of Queenes Celebrated". Similarly, when the Ingram-Swaim Milton concordance lists line 194 of *Comus* ("And envious darkness, ere they could return", in Douglas Bush's edition) under the HW THEY, the entry does not reveal that "they" is the subject of line 182 which reads, "My brothers, when they saw me wearied out". Nor is it reasonable to expect a concordance to supply such information: there are some inquiries which a printed concordance as an index cannot satisfy. It is easy to show why a concordance can never be more than an index. Early editors of concordances who worked from hand-printed or written slips had an opportunity to select an illustrative context to the works occurring in each line so as to optimize the information supplied under each different HW. So far as I can recall, no early concordance editor saw the necessity for this or came near to satisfying modern requirements. Bartlett, however, did vary the length of the illustrative contexts in his Shakespeare concordance, a function which is readily performed when the concordance is prepared by hand, but, clearly, he came to appreciate that there is a point beyond which illustrative contexts cannot extend if the size of the concordance is to remain within acceptable bounds. The ultimate possible context is when the complete works of an author is cited so as to illustrate the use of each of the words in it. This obvious *reductio ad absurdum* suggests that the concordance editor need only determine a more reasonable length of context in order to satisfy the users. However, what ultimately determines the "reasonableness" of the length of a contextual quotation is the nature of the specific inquiry addressed to the concordance; this, by and large, an editor can neither foresee nor anticipate. It is impossible for a concordance to supply a context suitable for any inquiry which may conceivably be made of it; consequently, a concordance must always be an index to texts which can be consulted in another place.

Two examples will make this clearer. Whereas the customary context for poetry concordances is a single verse, it would be valuable for the study of rhyme if the rhymed couplet were selected as the unit of illustrative context. Other more complex rhyming patterns, stanzaic or non-stanzaic, would require different lengths of contexts, but we can, at least for argument's sake, imagine a concordance in which the context was a unit of rhyme. However, a concordance arranged in such a way would be of little use for study of the sequence of the author's thought in patterns of images, nor would it aid study of the author's syntax, for each of which alternative optimum units of the context are conceivable. A context adequate for one kind of inquiry will not necessarily suit another. Further, some conceivable arrangements of concordances are possible only after the kind of analysis that the concordance itself was intended to aid. I can use the example of image clusters. Caroline Spurgeon cites six passages in Shakespeare which demonstrate an association of ideas and terms around "a dog or spaniel, fawning and licking; candy, sugar or sweets, thawing or melting".[28] A conventional alphabetized concordance would give a student small access to these six passages of Shakespeare unless he had a copy of Spurgeon's book at hand. She italicizes 29 words which form part of images associated with flattery and flatterers, but of the 20 lines of text which contain these terms, 13 lines contain two terms only. The concordance editor should therefore increase the context to two lines of text in order to improve the chances of illustrating an image cluster. However, 26 of the 29 words at which a user might start his inquiry into the "dog, sweets, melting" cluster would refer him to only a single passage noted by Spurgeon; a lengthened context would not help, save to suggest additional terms under which information may be sought. A conventional alphabetical listing of heading words with illustrative quotations would not provide ready access to Shakespeare's imagery, whereas any more sophisticated arrangement must perforce depend on just the kind of analysis which was carried out originally with the aid of Bartlett's concordance. One or the other of arrangement and analysis must come first. The concordance editor does not intend to analyse the text; rather, he sets out to prepare a general index as a working tool to aid any special analysis of the author's work. A concordance can offer only a structured means of access to the texts on which it is based; it is an index, not the work itself.

Furthermore, it is needful to assert for emphasis what no one would contemplate denying, that whatever the kind or length of context which is provided in the concordance, the user is not prevented from returning to the base text for an enlarged context. Indeed, it is my argument to this point that the concordance abstracts the base text and does not supersede it and this fundamental observation makes reference back to the base text unavoidable. I believe that modern concordance editors are sometimes unwarrantably defensive about the contexts which they supply.

In essence the concordance editor is obliged to judge what will suit the generality of his intended users: he seeks an "optimum" context where "optimum" is defined principally by the general requirements of users rather than by the specific form or function of the individual word being concorded. His decision will take heed of convenience of procedure and economy of publication. To the second of these considerations, at least, the would-be purchaser of the printed concordance would not be indifferent. When poetry is concorded, the verse line provides a convenient and acceptable context even though close scrutiny will reveal that many verses do not adequately illuminate the sense or diction of all the words in them. Again, it is unreasonable to expect that a concordance — the trespass of which into lexiographic domains must be sternly resisted — should supply such contexts. Concordance contexts give the "linguistic environment" of the occurrence of the particular word, an environment which may be typographic, prosodic, or syntactical, or a combination of these, and sometimes semantic. But that is infrequent, and not to be expected from the concordance, as I have shown before.

Whether the concordance editor can take account of it or not, different kinds of contexts are required by different classes of words. This observation is so obvious that it needs little discussion. Function words like pronouns, articles, and auxiliary verbs are best fitted with contexts which reveal the grammatical circumstances of their use, whereas for nouns, verbs, and their adjectival and adverbial modifiers, semasiological contexts are desirable. It is not likely that a context derived by a computer algorithm will accommodate such different requirements with equal success.

There has been a tendency in the literature of concording to regard novels and prose as requiring a rather different kind of context and, therefore, a different kind of context-determining algorithm, than concordances to verse. If it were true that contexts for verse and prose were essentially different, then the task of preparing a concordance of plays where prose and verse was mixed would be a hopeless one. Dr. J. E. G. Dixon, who gives the fullest recent discussion of context-generation techniques, writes that "Prose is characterized by two features, among others: variability of sentence structure, and variability of sentence length".[29] However, he does not show how these observations — which seem undeniably true and of equal application to prose and verse alike — impose special demands upon the editor of a concordance to prose works. So far as I can determine without technical aid from linguists, the most influential characteristic of prose in respect of contexts is that periods (and other syntactic units) tend to be longer in prose than in poetry, and they are longer more frequently, so that the concordance editor who attempts to supply a meaningful context must struggle constantly against the expansion of the concordance towards unusable bulk.[30] But, otherwise, the principles which govern the determination of a suitable context for a prose work seem exactly those which must be adopted for verse if the concordance editor's principal criterion for a context is revealed meaning rather than function or environment.[31] Dr. Dixon reacts strongly against the adoption of a typographical line as a context in the mistaken belief that it is more acceptable for verse than for prose. On the contrary, when the context is unsatisfactory, it is unsatisfactory regardless of whether the base text is poetry or prose. The use of a verse as a context in poetry is merely a convenience which the better manual concordances like Bartlett modified according to particular requirements.

Nevertheless, the use of a typographical line as a context does serve one important reference function. I am reminded of this when I recall my first attempts to use a concordance in which the typographical arrangement of prose differed in the text which I consulted from the text which had provided the base text for the concordance. It is very much more difficult to find the context in any book — when seeking more information about the circumstances of occurrence of a word — when the context and the lines of text do not start with the same words. (This phrasing covers two cases: when the context is not to typographical lines, and when the arrangement of the consulted text is different from that of the concorded text.) The difficulty is compounded when the reference is not exact, to a chapter, say, rather than to lines which are numbered in the text referred to (like the Conrad concordance mentioned above). In such a case it is desirable for the concordance editor to ensure either that the context commences at the beginning of a typographical line in the base text, or includes a line-beginning which is clearly marked, in the fashion of the recent Shakespeare concordances. In each case the user should be made aware of the concordance's practice by the editor's introduction, for the practice adopted will affect the manner in which readers will use the concordance.

In their search for the optimum context concordance editors have used devices which (a) fill a context field of predetermined length, as in some KWIC concordance formats, or which (b) do not fill the context field. The context field is of fixed length even in a manual concordance, the concordancer invariably having determined that no context can extend beyond, say, two lines, but the use of the context field may be variable. The *Harvard Shakespeare Concordance,* for example, uses a fixed-length context field of 48 characters but does not fill it when the algorithm (which determines the extent of the context syntactically) produces a context line "Ay." which is less than 48 characters.[32]

Furthermore, in relation to the typographical layout of the base texts, contexts are (c) variable in extent, or (d) of fixed length, the length being determined by the typographical arrangement of the base text. I have said enough about this latter case not to pursue it further. There is some interest, however, in discussion of how modern concordance editors, having fettered their wills to the machine, have attempted to regain the innocent freedom of the manual concordance editor to suit the context to the word.

Computer-extracted Contexts

Computer-extracted contexts may be produced by three general methods.

Pre-editing

At the pre-editing stage of data preparation the introduction of context-delimiting symbols is intended to identify the best contexts to the computer which will generate them automatically thereafter, with suppression of the editing characters.[33] This is a far more sophisticated and laborious procedure than the simple attachment of short lines to preceding lines in order to avoid the incongruity of unusually short and hence unrevealing contexts, but it does result in a high percentage of "meaningful" contexts. The text — as Dr. Dixon shows in the most explicit description of the pre-editing method I have encountered (op. cit.) — is divided into syntactical units which are taken to be meaningful in respect of the main words in them although in particular instances the meaning or sense of the context may not be lucid even though the syntax is. The main advantage of this method is that the concordance editor works directly from the base text and has available to him the fullest possible range of information from which to anticipate the needs of users. A substantial disadvantage — which is not peculiar to this method — is that the contexts are continuous and sequential: there is no provision for the omission of words in such a period as the concordance editor will have to refer continually to the base text and may need to add context to the computer record. This is an awkward expedient likely to produce error.

Lexicographers like Father Busa use an extensive context of many lines from which they can extract (manually) the appropriate quotation designed to illustrate the meaning or use of the particular word. Dr. Tollenaere describes a "highly flexible context of approximately six or seven lines, constituting a fair unity from a syntactic point of view" generated by the computer.[36] The concordance editor's position is similar to that of the lexicographer who examines contexts to determine their usefulness for dictionary citation: in each case the computer-abstracted context must be regarded as raw data for the publishable index. Yet I do not advocate that the concordance editor scrutinize an extended context: that would be unbearably onerous for a large corpus, and, as I have shown, the function of a concordance and a lexicon is distinct: the contextual requirements are necessarily distinct also. A computer algorithm which generates a concordance context designed to fill a fixed-length field will produce satisfactory concordance contexts in the greatest number of cases. It would be advantageous, however, for the contexts which are not adequate, if the concordance editor had automatic access to an extended context. I am suggesting here that two contexts should be generated for each entry: (i) a fixed-length short context designed for publication, in the style of the Spevack Shakespeare concordances, and (ii) and extensive lexicographic context designed for the use of the concordance editor in the post-editing phase of concordance generation. The extensive context would not be printed out. I conceive that in future concordance editors will seek to edit alphabetized concordance data with the aid of visual display units and special editing programmes. In that event I envisage that the editor will survey the short publishable contexts of the VDU, and when an inadequate context appears, he will summon up visual display of the extended context which he will then edit and substitute for the original short context. In such a case — which would be relatively infrequent — there would be no need to observe a fixed-field limitation which was determined by the requirement that a single entry in the concordance must occupy a single line in the published concordance, because the final publication programme — as the Oxford Shakespeare

Concordances show — will have the capacity of turning over-long context lines into a second line of print.[37]

In the foregoing discussion I have assumed the most extreme optimization of syntactical contexts. Concordance contexts can be "meaningful", I suggest, only on the level of syntax; more extensive semasiological contexts do not lie within the function of the concordance to provide. If that is an agreeable position then the most acceptable contexts may be computer-generated with a high probability of suitability if the extent of the context to be published is determined not by the format of the published concordance but by some such consideration as the average length of readily defined syntactical units in the base text. Very often only arduous and time-consuming experimentation will provide an optimal computer concordance context algorithm.

Problems of Linearity

The discussion of context already is so complicated that I shrink from the introduction of further complexity, but there are additional problems created by complex, that is, non-linear, texts which need to be acknowledged even though I am not aware of concordances to such texts. I use the text of Ben Jonson's plays to illustrate these problems which are frequent in works of the earlier periods.

When a literary text is read into the computer, it is input card by card, line by line, sequentially, or it is read from a paper tape on which the text has been punched word by word, line by line, unit by unit, serially. The computer operates on the text in similar fashion, responding to different features to the text according to its programmed instructions, but generally proceeding progressively from the start to the end of the texts it has been set to work on. The output for a concordance is arranged sequentially, with entries set out beneath HWs which run from A to Z. However extensive the context illustrating the occurrence of a particular word might be, it is usually linear in form. Unlike the definitive edition on which it may be based, the concordance contains no marginal notes, linear glosses, textual collations or footnotes, or references to information printed elsewhere. Although frequency counts, separate concordances to special classes of texts or words, and the like may be printed after the main alphabetical sequence, each section is integral and linear in structure. It is neither desirable nor possible for a concordance to reproduce the arrangement of text on such an illustrative page of Jonson's as p. 975 of the 1616 Folio, the first page of the masque, *Oberon the Fairy Prince* (Fig. 4). Nor can the concordance editor justifiably resolve his difficulties by the decision to omit the marginal notes, or to concord them in an appendix, corresponding to solutions adopted by recent editors of the text. He assumes that every word of the text is germane to the author's literary record and that none is dispensable on mere formal grounds. Yet he has two problems. The printed text is spatial and non-sequential lineally, and he must translate the given sequence of lines and glosses into the lineal mode on which the computer can operate. He needs must do this within the constraints of technology which did not evolve to suit his purposes. Printing presses were designed to print books, but computers were not designed for the production of concordances. Secondly, he must decide how the marginal notes should be linked to the text to which they refer. This question leads him to consider what length of context is suitable either for words in the main text, or for the marginal notes, or both.

It is possible that the best procedure will arise from experimentation especially with complex arrangements of the main text. In Jonson's *Bartholomew Fair,* for example, there is a song, beside which are set three speeches of 6, 4, and 2 lines respectively; to the right of the speeches is printed a long marginal stage direction. Any conceivable arrangement of this portion of the text for concording must be merely a compromise, and the concordance editor will hope that in a definitive edition the arrangement is simplified, at least to the extent of inserting the stage direction in the main body of the text. Otherwise it might not be possible to provide in the concordance either an efficient context or correct line numbering. Some stage directions are printed between lines of text to which they apply as in the *Case is Altered* at 1.6.80:

$$\textit{Servants} \left\{ \begin{array}{l} \text{Signior Paulo} \\ \text{Lord Ferneze} \end{array} \right\} \quad \textit{within.}$$

or 1.6.91-3

$$\textit{within.} \left\{ \begin{array}{l} \textit{Count} \ldots \\ \textit{Christ} \ldots \\ \textit{Count} \ldots \end{array} \right.$$

SATYRE. I.

CHROMIS, [b] MNASYL? None appeare?
  See you not, who riseth here?
    [c] You saw SILENVS, late, I feare!
  I'le proue, if this can reach your eare.

a b They are the names of two yong *Satyres*, I find in *Vir. Eclog.6.* that took *Silenus* sleeping; who is fain'd to bee the *Pedigree* of *Bacchus* : As the *Satyres* are his Collusores, or

Play-fellowes. So doth *Dioder Siculus*, *Synesius*, *Julian, in Cæsarib* report them.   c A prouerbiall speech, when they will taxe one the other of drinking, or sleepinesse ; alluding to that former place, *in Virgil. Chromis & Mnasyles in antro Silenum, pueri, somno videre iacentem*, Inflatum besterno venas, ut semper Iaccho.

He wound his Cornet, and thought himselfe answer'd; but was deceiued by the Echo.

O, you wake then: Come away,
  Times be short, are made for play ;
  The hum'rous Moone too will not stay:
  What doth make you thus delay ?
[d] Hath his tankard touch'd your braine ?
  Sure, they' ar falne asleepe againe :
  Or I doubt it was the vaine
  Echo, did me entertaine.

d *Silenus* is euery where made a louer of wine, as in *Cyclope Eurip* and known by that notable ensigne, his tankard : out of the same place of *Virg. Et grauis attritâ pendebat cantharus ansâ.* As also out of that famous piece of sculpture, in a little gem or piece of *Iasper*, obseru'd by *Monsieur Caufabon*, in his tract *de Saty.*

vitâ poësi, from *Rascasius Bagarrius* : wherein is described the whole manner of the *Scene*, and *eben*, of *Bacchus*, with *Silenus*, and the *Satyres*. An elegant and curious antiquitie, both for the subtiltie and labour : where, in so small a compasse, (to vse his words) there is *Rerum, Personarum, Actionum plane stupenda varietas.*

Proue againe. I thought 'twas shee.   { *He wound the second*
  Idle *Nymph*, I pray thee, bee   { *time, and found it.*
  Modest, and not follow me :
[e] I nor loue my selfe, nor thee.

e Respecting that knowne fable of *Echo's* following *Narcissus*; and his selfe-Loue.

Here he wound the third time, and was answer'd by another Satyre, *who likewise shewed himselfe. To which he spoke.*

I, this sound I better know:
  List ! I would I could heare mo.
At this they came running forth seuerally, from diuers parts of the Rocke, leaping, and making antique action, and gestures, to the number of tenne ; some

Nnnn 2

of

Fig. 4. Ben Jonson's *Works*, 1616, p. 975: the first page of *Oberon The Fairy Prince*, an extreme example of non-linearity in a text to be concorded.

and a similar example at 4.7.47-8 where "Within." brackets two speeches on the right. The spatial arrangement of the printed text cannot be preserved in the concordance where, after the text is transposed into a linear mode, the editor must supply correct line references to the source text. Nevertheless, one can suggest a means of dealing with such complex arrangements of the text. The plays, and sometimes the masques, contain marginal stage directions. In the *Sad Shepherd* at 2.2.37, "Hee/drawes/out other/presents." is an example (*H&S*, vii, p. 29). Whether these occur in the original to the right or, as in 2.6 in Herford and Simpson's edition, for example, to the left of the page, the marginal stage direction will be attached to the line of text alongside which it commences, the lineation of the base text will be indicated, and the line number will be that of the base line. The whole context line (or lines, depending on what length of context is judged suitable) will be printed in the concordance under the headings for each of the words which occurs in it.

A different method may be followed with the marginal notes in which Jonson supplied information and references to his sources in support of the main text. These notes are usually indicated in the text by superior numbers or letters, but sometimes they are not superior, or are absent. Regardless of the arrangement of notes and text adopted by an editor of the text; the concordance editor must adopt a consistent procedure, and he may introduce into the computer-readable text nonce references which may or may not, as he decides, be printed in the published concordance. The computer can be instructed to recognize the beginning of marginal notes if consistent indications, like superior characters, are present, but the computer cannot detect to what words in the text the notes refer in the absence of such distinguishing characters. Each marginal note should follow the line to which it applies; upon the detection in the base line of the character which indicates an accompanying marginal note (i.e. the superior character or the like), the concordance programme will take both the base line (or lines) and the whole marginal note following it as the unit of illustrative context. Notes like notes *a* and *b* in the page of *Oberon the Fairy Prince* illustrated relate to single words in the base line; others, like note *d*, gloss the whole line of text. Many marginal notes are long, and to use the base line together with the complete marginal note as the context for each of the words in the base line would increase the length of the concordance unacceptably. Alternative procedures are not easy to devise. A method suggested by notes *a* and *b* in *OFP* would be to attach the marginal note to the base line as context only under the heading of the annotated word; that is, the line "aCHROMIS, bMNASYL? None appeare?" *and* the whole of note *a, b* would be printed under the heading words CHROMIS and MNASYL, while under NONE and APPEARE, only the base line would be printed as context. (A user curious about the content of the notes, which he would see indicated by superscript letters, would know to seek access to the notes under the respective superscripted HWs.) This method would not, however, be suitable for note *d* in the illustration since the superscripted word is "Hath" which belongs to that class of frequently occurring words which may not be provided with illustrative contexts in the concordance. The difficulty could be resolved if the computer were programmed to associate the note as context with the first word in the base line not so included on a list of words not to be supplied with full contexts. It would be possible to add such an entry a legend like "For the notes, *see* under TANKARD" so as not to impose a burden of reference on the user.

Other concording problems arise from the length of the notes, and the character of the information contained in them. Some of the notes to the stanzas of Jonson's *Masque of Queens* extend to around 150 words; the verses average about seven words in length. This is a long tail for a small dog. Any alternative solution creates greater awkwardnesses. If the length of context were to be limited to any set number of words it would be difficult to decide how to dispose of the rest of the note. The notes contain passages in many languages and supply not only glossorial information and commentary on the text, but also bibliographical references to Jonson's sources. Much of this information must be considered intrusive in a concordance to the works of an English author for, if it did nothing else, its presence in the main concordance sequence would contaminate any counts of frequency of words the editor chose to supply. This could be avoided if the notes, which would be entered in the concordance under the HW to which they applied, were otherwise to be ignored. However, another, and, I think, a sounder solution to the problem of the notes, can be suggested word in any fashion.

The word field in most concordances is variable in position; only in KWIC/KWOC concordances does it become fixed in position.

Text Sigla

Unless the concordance is to a single work, in which case there will ordinarily be no sigil, the title of the texts referred to in the entries will be denoted by sigla. The length of the sigla is determined mainly by the size of the field in the printed entry allotted to accommodate it: in the Ingram-Swaim Milton concordance the sigla range from "Par Lost" to "Mask" within an eight-character field. The Harvard Shakespeare concordance used the conventional contractions for the titles of Shakespeare's works: these are restricted to three characters exclusive of the period denoting contraction, as in *Tim.*

When a recognized and generally accepted system of reference to titles by contractions exists, as it does for Shakespeare, the concordance editor would be ill advised to devise his own system. When he needs to, however, he must take account of the necessity of the contractions to be readily memorized: the sigla must have the mnemonic property of summoning up the full title of the work referred to. The contraction *Den.* would not do for the play of *Hamlet, Prince of Denmark,* for instance. There is usually a strong tendency towards conciseness of reference — a character position saved in the sigla field may allow the context field to be expanded — but conciseness conflicts with the demands of clarity and exclusivity. The sigil must denote a single text clearly but only one text in the author's canon: no ambiguity can be permitted. It is on that account that the old sigil for *Titus Andronicus (TA)* was superseded by *Tit.* The user could never be sure whether it was *Titus Andronicus* or *Timon of Athens* that was referred to without recourse to a table of abbreviations.

The character of the abbreviations for the titles of texts is significant for another reason. When the concorded entries are sorted for listing beneath the appropriate HWs, the order of entries which relate to different texts is usually determined by the sigla which denote the text titles. The entries for *Much Ado about Nothing,* to use another Shakespearian example, would appear in different sequence according to whether the new sigil *Ado.* was sorted on, or whether the concordance editor used the old convention, *MAN; KL* and *Lr., KJ* and *Jn.* give further examples. The sigla are of more far-reaching importance in concording than the novice concordance editor might pause to consider.[40]

The best position for the text sigil is preceding the reference to the part of the work where the entry may be consulted, i.e., before the text reference field.

Text Reference Field

The last item of information required by the user as he seeks information relevant to his inquiry, from the HW through the context to the titles of the separate works, is a precise reference to the spot in the text where he can locate the context. Although the details of the reference are determined by the character of the particular work, the order of reference is generally from the largest compositional unit (e.g. act, book, chapter) through any intermediate unit (e.g., scene, canto, paragraph) to the specific line. The system of references is determined for the concordance by the organization or literary structure of the base work.

The essential requirement of the text reference field is that the system of reference permits the entries under a single HW to appear in sequential order of the base text. This point is important enough to be stressed; the entries beneath the HWs should occur in the order in which the user will naturally access the base text. In a play, entries from act one will be followed by entries for act two and so on, the individual contexts from each act being listed in numerical order of lines. The absence of such order of entries is a considerable blemish in a concordance: no more effective inhibition upon the effective use of a concordance in relation to its base text can be imagined than an apparently random sequence of entries. (This observation has especial force in relation to KWIC indexes: q.v.) Inexpert concordance editors sometimes adopt alpha-numerical text references like III.3.126 which sort the entries into an undesirable order which requires another sort to correct.

Principles of authority, economy, and clarity apply to the text references as to the sigla. Simplicity is commendable to ease the reader's eyes. Generally roman numerals separated by spaces or periods, e.g. 3.6.32 or 3 6 32, work best within the confines of a reference field which is usually kept to minimum extent in order to provide the fullest possible context field.

There is a question sometimes as to what precisely the text reference refers — the whole context or the location of the concorded word. To avoid confusion, the general principle seems sound that the reference supplies the location of the concorded *word* in the base text. Moreover, some concordances endeavour to attain a general utility by the adoption of a system of reference which applies not to a single specific edition (the base text) but to all existing and any conceivable future editions of the author's works. This unfortunate practice of omission of line references has a long history in connection with Shakespearian concordances, being found in the first Shakespeare concordance, Andrew Becket's *A Concordance to Shakespeare suited to all the Editions,* published in 1787. It would not be surprising to find somewhere in the dusty stacks of a research library a dramatic concordance in which the editor eschewed references to scenes in order to mitigate the effects of disagreement over scene divisions amongst current editions. A concordance which attempts to refer to everything in general succeeds only in referring to nothing in particular.

On the other hand, other concordances supply more than one system of reference: the Erdman Blake concordance gives references to the base edition (Sir Geoffrey Keynes's *Complete Writings,* 1957) by page number, and also to Blake's work by title, section, and line number as appropriate. A similar form of double entry to both the source text (Eugene Vinaver's 1967 edition of the Winchester manuscript) by page and line numbers and the compositional sections of the work (Caxton's book and chapter divisions) is used in Tomomi Kato's *A Concordance to the Works of Sir Thomas Malory* (Tokyo, 1974). The Dylan Thomas concordance prepared by R. C. Williams gives "page, line and poem number references as they appear in the editions published in the United Kingdom (J. M. Dent) and in the United States (New Directions)".[41] References tied to a specific modern edition of the works — or an old one for that matter — are useful only while those editions are generally available. If the modern edition is subsequently reprinted with different pagination from the previous edition, the references lose much of their usefulness. Nevertheless, the user retains access to the works themselves from the alternative references to divisions of the works: these usually do not vary greatly from edition to edition.

Frequency Counts

Some concordances supply a count of the individual occurrences of the lemmatized word contained in the entries beneath the HW. The best position for a count is the HW line, a position which saves many lines of type and therefore much paper by the avoidance of a separate line for the count. The value of the count depends mainly on the extent to which homographs are distinguished and the HW refers to entries which illustrate the occurrence of a single word only. Much depends upon how the "word" itself is defined, as Dr. W. Ingram justly points out.[42] When the HW relates to a mass of undifferentiated entries in the manner discussed in the section on *Homograph distinction,* the frequency counts serve little useful purpose, although it should be noticed that not all HWs refer to a mixture of homographs: a concordance to a text in modern spelling will give useful counts for many function words like "it, there, we, was, of", which are rarely homographic.

Other Information

The Harvard Shakespeare concordance uses the HW line to record the frequency count by occurrences in prose and verse contexts, and prints a figure which gives the relative frequency of the concorded word in relation to the total number of words in the individual work or whole canon. The different kinds of information which could be added to the basic form of entry clearly depend on the characteristics of the works to be concorded, the ingenuity of the concordance editor to devise and supply, and usual considerations of what value such information might have for the general reader. Just so long as the fundamental alphabetical order of HWs and text order of entries is not

MACBETH

```
HASTE see also hast = 1
  Lenox. What a haste lookes through his eyes?                        69
HAT = 1
  Malc. Mercifull Heauen: | What man, ne're pull your hat vpon your
  browes:                                                          2054
HATCHD = 1
  New hatch'd toth' wofull time.                                    808
HATE = 2
  Speake then to me, who neyther begge, nor feare | Your fauors, nor
  your hate.                                                        160
  Some say hee's mad: Others, that lesser hate him, | Do call it valiant
  Fury, but for certaine                                           2190
HATEFULL = 1
  *Y.Sey. The diuell himselfe could not pronounce a Title | More hatefull
  to mine eare.                                                    2406
HATH l.*94 180 193 243 271 434 442 *460 491 505 508 513 587 *648 649
  699 732 819 820 917 928 954 1007 1043 1089 1099 1111 1198 1201 1290
  1322 *1347 1441 1511 1528 1598 *1829 1891 1912 1914 1940 1943 1946
  1974 1989 2030 2458 2492 = 45*7
HAUE l.112 124 126 137 186 224 255 283 303 313 316 *349 *350 *357 369
  370 377 382 408 443 464 482 499 *504 508 518 532 533 536 538 557 559
  *572 594 597 615 654 659 665 709 *745 *748 *760 792 895 926 *1006
  1020 1055 1056 1070 1102 1164 1167 1175 1221 1249 1316 1349 1360
  1386 1403 1404 *1405 1406 1422 1432 1440 1473 *1475 1487 1713 1782
  1795 1800 1826 1828 1841 1863 1867 1897 *1917 1921 1929 1955 1981
  2022 2035 2045 2061 *2095 *2098 *2106 *2122 *2131 2139 *2146 *2150
  *2151 2184 2219 2221 2239 2243 2306 2314 2326 2330 2331 2334 2338
  2339 2343 2396 2432 2441 2444 2465 2496 = 100*22
HAUING = 3*1
  Of Noble hauing, and of Royall hope,                              156
  The Interim hauing weigh'd it, let vs speake | Our free Hearts each to
  other.                                                            272
  And my more-hauing, would be as a Sawce                          1906
  *Gent. Neither to you, nor any one, hauing no witnesse           2110
HAUNT = 2
  Where they must breed, and haunt: I haue obseru'd                 443
  My Wife and Childrens Ghosts will haunt me still:                2418
HAUNTING = 1
  Banq. This Guest of Summer, | The Temple-haunting Barlet does
  approue,                                                          437
HAUTBOYES see hoboyes, ho-boyes
HAWKT = 1
  Was by a Mowsing Owle hawkt at, and kill'd.                       939
HAY = 1
  I'th' Ship-mans Card. | Ile dreyne him drie as Hay:              115
HAYLD = 1
  They hayl'd him Father to a Line of Kings.                       1050
HAYLE = 3
  1. Hayle. | 2. Hayle. | 3. Hayle.                                 162
HE see also hee, hee's, he's = 102*8
HEAD = 9
  And fix'd his Head vpon our Battlements.                          42
```

Fig. 5. *Macbeth*, p. 95 of the *Oxford Shakespeare Concordance*. Notice the references (haste, hautboyes, he), the count-only word (he), the location-only words (hath, haue), the context with multiple occurrences of the concorded word (hayle), and the asterisk denoting a long line in the original edition. There is no text identifier since only a single text is concorded, and the text reference is in the form of a consecutive count of typographical lines in the base text. The arrangement is by old spellings.

tampered with, there is no limitation to what additional information could be supplied. Entries in the Oxford Shakespeare concordances use an asterisk before the entry to show that the line of context extended to the full extent of the compositor's measure in the base text (Fig. 5), with possible effect on the spellings in that line: that is a special device in a concordance intended for specialist users which is not advocated for more general application. Nevertheless, I have many times thought that in a concordance to plays it would assist the user if he was informed of the name of the character who spoke the speech, with the name printed as part of the context. It is easy to multiply possibilities for useful information but it is not generally easy to devise the means by which the information can be abstracted from the text.

KWIC Concordance Formats

One form of concordance arrangement which is frequently found on account of the wide dispersion of programmes is the *Key-Word-In Context* index first described by Hans Luhn in 1959.[43] Luhn was concerned to provide access to technical literature by automatic indexing of the terms in the titles of articles and similar bibliographical material. Although he was clearly aware of the similarity of the KWIC process to conventional concordance making — IBM Form E20-8091 notices that "The process may be applied to either the title, abstract, or entire text of a document" (p. 3) — Luhn's main concern was to devise a system of reference to bibliographical titles which, like the literature of chemistry, are characterized by a high density of index terms. Such terms as function words not likely to be useful for subject access were suppressed in the alphabetical sequence of entries.

The development of KWIC indexes contributes a minor irony to the history of technology and literary scholarship. Technical literature may be concorded conventionally just as readily as any other kind of literature, but the citations under the index terms would range from the merely casual and relatively uninformative to the most significant and definitive. In any event, the bulk of a single-volume or periodically published concordance to the literature of, say, chemistry, would render its use inefficient and costly. However, the titles to technical articles usually define precisely the areas of their essential concern, and an index term forming part of a title would relate to a significant body of information within the bibliographical item itself. It was a significant advance in information retrieval when Luhn observed that conventional concordance techniques could be applied not only to texts but also to titles of documents. On the other hand, history does not record who was the first prospective concordance editor to approach his computer centre for assistance, to be informed of the KWIC programme which might, with a little adjustment here and there, be bent to the purpose of literary concordance making. The irony is that a general concordance programme which was rewritten to facilitate special technical indexing is now widely used again, after special modification, for general concording of literary texts.

As one might expect from the adaptation of a specialized tool for a general function, KWIC concordances are often not very efficient. It is difficult to generalize because there are many modifications of the original conception; indeed, it may be true that KWIC concordances differ amongst themselves rather more conspicuously than conventional concordances. The original and to some extent essential characteristics of the KWIC index are these: although there are no HWs, the indexed terms within the alphabetized sequence of citations are delimited within their contexts. As Miss Campey puts it: "The KWIC format is achieved by aligning keywords and the associated text on a particular volume so that their alphabetic sequence can be readily observed" (p. 9). The context is limited to a number of characters within a single line of input or output, the full extent determined by the number of character positions allocated to the reference field. The keywords (the indexed terms) can be positioned anywhere in the line and accordingly the context can be restricted to what follows or succeeds the keyword; the common format is to print keywords in a column in the centre of the context field with the context filling up the remaining character positions before and after it.

In the first form of KWIC index, the index occupied the first part: alphabetized index entries with a small extent of defining context referred (by a compact reference to the right of each entry) to full bibliographical citations of the documents which were printed in a separate sequence from the KWIC index. The citations might be arranged by authors, or document numbers, or any other useful order

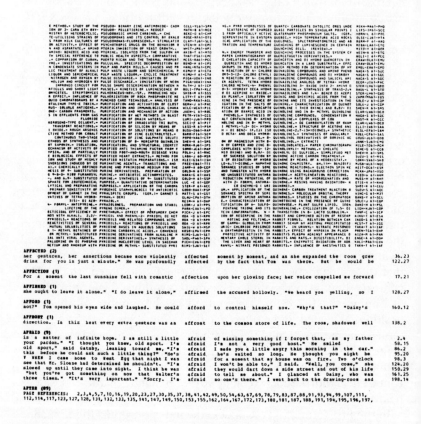

Fig. 6. KWIC indexes (a) to technical literature, and (b) literary text: *A Concordance to F. Scott Fitzgerald's The Great Gatsby,* comp. by Andrew T. Crosland. Detroit, 1976. Note the wrap-around context in (a) but the suppression of normal KWIC features in (b).

according to the system of reference printed in the reference field. However, if the KWIC index used a concordance programme, the function of the second part is undertaken by the base text, but this is not usually printed with the index. A variant of the KWIC index is the pretentiously named *Key-Word-Out-of-Context* index, in which the HW is printed at the left of the page at the head of a sequence of entries: this is the conventional concordance format. Despite the implication the keyword remains in context as usual (Fig. 6).[44]

KWIC indexes are subject to a variation called "Double-KWIC" in which "The first significant word in a title (main term) is extracted, and then the remaining significant words are rotated and displayed under the main term (subordinate entries). The index entries are sorted alphabetically by main term and within this sequence by subordinate terms."[45] Although I am not aware of an English concordance which adopts this procedure, it is not uncommon to find KWIC concordances in which the entries relating to a single keywork are alphabetically sorted on a secondary field of characters which precede or succeed the keyword (the primary sort field).[46] The benefit sought from such an arrangement of entries is the enhanced opportunity to observe significant collocation of terms which is possible for literature (like Latin or technical bibliography) with a high density of indexable terms. The protagonists of second-field sorting rarely consider its disadvantages for concordances of English literary works which are characterized by frequent occurrences of words of low semantic content, e.g. articles, prepositions, and pronouns. In the following artificial example, in which the first term is the keyword, there are as many relatively useless as relatively useful immediate collocations; if one imagines the example expanded by many more entries, it is easy to see how the sequence does (or need not: ONE was selected at random) effectively collocate significant terms in the manner claimed for the secondary sorting process:

It is possible to object to secondary sorting because it does not accomplish what it pretends to accomplish but, as the example reveals at a glance, there is a further substantial objection to second-field sorting which applies to KWIC indexes in general.

... One day 891
... One day's work 78
... One fair day 102
... One fair day's work 740
... One fat pig 632
... One of the fair days 7
... One of the fat pigs 338
... One of these days 221
... One of those pigs 202
... One! Off with 43
... One on the fat 783
... One the pig 621
... One pig 948
... One work-day 75

The essential objections to KWIC indexes are two; the first is crucial.
(1) In basic KWIC indexes there is no sort on the reference field.
Accordingly, in a KWIC index to a number of different texts and to
single texts when there is secondary sorting, the order of citations is
not that of the base text. In the original KWIC indexes designed for
technical information retrieval, in the whole KWIC index there would
be a mere handful of entries to each single document, and the user of
the index, having selected the document references which seemed
most promising for his purpose, expected to access them document by
document. On the other hand, in the KWIC concordance there are a
large number of entries, all or any important number of which may be
pertinent to the user's inquiry, which refer to a handful or so of texts
which the user normally expects to find printed in a single edition. In
order to use the references from the KWIC concordance efficiently
the user must transcribe and sort them into text order, a process
normally undertaken by the computer. The alternative — virtually
random entry to the base text — is scarcely to be contemplated with
equanimity.

In rebuttal, protagonists of KWIC concordances may claim that the
user need never consult the base text because the KWIC contexts are

so generous in extent. This is intrinsically unlikely, as the previous discussion has shown, but in any event the context supplies the second heading under which KWIC concordances are vulnerable to criticism. (2) KWIC contexts are completely arbitrary; they fill a context field of predetermined length merely, without consideration of how well they fill it. Such a method is adequate for titles of technical articles with their special high-density syntax but is seriously defective for more diffuse literary works. Furthermore, line endings are not generally indicated in the context, and the user does not have the guidance of being able to refer to the beginnings of verse or typographical lines when he seeks a context more extensive than that supplied in the KWIC concordance.

Notwithstanding, there are KWIC concordances already published which are not vulnerable to criticisms such as these. However, they are concordances produced by programmes in which the distinctive KWIC features were suppressed in order to return the KWIC index to its origin, the conventional concordance.

CHAPTER 5

COMPREHENSIVENESS

HAVING considered the fundamental organization of the concordance we can now examine the controversial question of what should be included in the main arrangement. In the simplest form of concordance, complete texts go into the computer and every word in them is accorded exactly the same treatment: the capacity of the machine for undiscriminating reproduction of material is used to the full. It was not always so. The merely human editors of the early concordances more often than not supplied entries for only the words they took to be more significant in their texts, and very often they gave only a selection of "representative" illustrations of their use. Gradually, since scholarship abhors a vacuum, the selective concordances became superseded by comprehensive — or at least more comprehensive — concordances. The growing interest in the statistical analysis of language in this century led almost inevitably to demands for concordances in which every occurrence of every word in a corpus of writings was represented in the concordance. Concordances finally achieved — in the precursor of the Harvard Shakespeare concordance, for example — what editors who worked from slips shrank from but which the computer could scarcely avoid: a full entry for every word in the base text.

The strongest argument for the provision of an illustrative context for every occurrence of every word in the concorded text is supplied by the necessities of literary statistics. Statistics are considered in the following chapter, but it should be mentioned that there are many statistical observations which cannot be made if frequency counts are not available for all words. Amongst students of Shakespeare's language one of the severest criticisms of Bartlett's concordance (1894) was its omission both of frequency counts and of information pertaining to a substantial portion of Shakespeare text through the omission of a large number of common words.

On the other hand, in any literary work there are words which occur so frequently that it has seemed to many concorders almost supererogatory to list contexts for them: words like *a* and *the* for example. The virtue of listing such words is that a reader will have all the evidence for his inquiry laid out before him in one place. However frequent the word is in the text, the computer at least will have not overlooked a single occurrence. Nevertheless, the number of readers interested in *a, the, it,* and so on will not be great; if the concordancer has not himself considered the economies which might be achieved by the omission of contexts for such words, his publisher will. It is easy to sympathize with Dr. Spevack's rejection of the claims of economy at the expense of scholarly objectivity.[47] Nevertheless, it is possible to assert a distinction between what should be published in hard covers for the great variety of users, and what other information may be made available for special purposes, in a variety of forms. One could go so far as to consider a published concordance which is as complete as Dr. Spevack advocates a special form of concordance.[48]

Notwithstanding, it is important to resist the conclusion that "frequency is directly proportional to unimportance".[49] Although the greatest economies in the bulk of a published concordance will be accomplished by the omission of entries for the most frequent words, it should not be economy which determines the omission but the significance of the word in the works of the author being concorded. In practice the distinction is between high-frequency words which are semantically significant (e.g. *will* n.) and those which are syntactically important (e.g. *will* v.). The Harvard Shakespeare concordance omits contexts for the following words: *the, and, I, to, of, a, you, my, that, in, is, not, me, for, it, with, be, his, this, your, he, but, have, as, thou, so, him, will, what, her, thy, no, all, by, do, shall, if, are, we, thee, our, on, now.*

These words, which, except for *as, all* and *now,* were also given without contexts in the Oxford Shakespeare concordances, were the "first forty-three words in order of frequency in Shakespeare".[50] The syntactical basis for the exclusion of most of these words is fairly clear, although, when it came to the point, the Harvard editor could find no satisfactory definition of "significance": "The soundest principle [for exclusion] — the clearest and most objective — seemed the quantitative".[51]

The concordance editor will not be able to avoid the problem of significance in this connection. His best guide is his appreciation of the main characteristics of his author's language, an appreciation which preparation of the concordance itself will enhance. Like the Harvard Shakespeare concordance, Lane Cooper's Wordsworth concordance includes contexts for *like* but omits them for *as,* for economy but to the detriment of the study of the poetic rhetoric. In concordances to plays an unidentified *I* has little but formal significance; in the works of poets like Emily Dickinson and Dylan Thomas entries under that heading may come near to illustrating the writers' poetic biography or persona.[52]

In printed concordances words which are represented by frequency counts alone throw the concordance reader back on his own resources, unless information on those words is provided in another form, like computer printout or microfiche. The number of such words should be as small as possible. Desirable restriction can be achieved by establishing a second list of words which are provided both with frequency counts and line references in place of the full contexts. This device, which was adopted in the Oxford Shakespeare concordances and the Freeman and Batson Racine concordance,[53] is economical for words of relatively high frequency and low semantic value, whilst it enables the user to locate all occurrences of each word with only moderate difficulty.

In summary, the concordance editor cannot be oblivious to the claims of economy, either of the cost of computation or publication. Favourable economic conditions and the importance of an author such as Shakespeare may justify the most comprehensive kind of concordance. Economy apart, there is certainly no harm in printing pages of context for *a, the,* and similar words when the author's canon is not extensive, but for authors as voluminous as Shaw and Dickens and other nineteenth-century novelists, the great bulk of entries under the most common syntactical terms, with the attendant cost of printing and publishing and the likelihood that those sections of the concordance would attract only scant use, must yield to economy. Nevertheless, economics must be tempered by consideration of the significance of the words which are candidates for exclusion by virtue of their frequency. Ultimately, what the concordance editor publishes must be justified by the kind and extent of use which it is reasonable to envisage for the concordance.

Whatever are the words set apart for special treatment in the published concordance the concordance editor must ensure that homographs of them are distinguished (e.g. *might* n./*might* v.) and other special uses of the word reserved for full entry. There are two methods of marking instances of common words for full listing. Very often a line-printed version of the concordance, in which every word is supplied with full contexts, is read for the distinction of entries. However, experience shows that simple scanning of numerous entries under a single heading often hypnotizes a reader so that the exceptional usage of the term is overlooked. Consequently, the better practice is to tag homographs or special instances when the text is being prepared (by pre-editing) for input. Serial reading keeps the editor awake, and distinctive usages are more readily noticed in the context of the whole text than in the often severely limited concordance context. The manner of treating the special instances after their separation depends mainly on the overall design of the concordance. It is important, however, that principles and procedures are drawn prominently to the reader's attention in the introduction to the published concordance.

Foreign Language

Foreign language material poses separate problems of inclusion. Sometimes it is difficult to determine whether the words are foreign or not: *depot* may now be regarded as "Frenglish" but *depôt* as still French. Distinction may be made, on the evidence of context, with the guide of a historical dictionary like the *OED* and its supplements. At stake here is the integrity of whatever statistics may be provided: only suspect conclusions about the relationship of an author's language to the language of his time can be drawn from figures based on an undiscriminating mixture of a variety of languages. The plays of Ben Jonson again provide an illustration of the problem.

Jonson used Latin (in phrases throughout the plays and extensively in marginal notes to the masques), Greek, French, Spanish, Italian, German, Welsh, Dutch, and Irish: in some texts, especially his masques, the non-English passages make up a significant portion of the whole text. Consequently, for a Jonson concordance the different languages require to be identified for the computer by the addition of a tag during pre-editing. When the concordance programme met the tag during its serial passage through the text, it would add the appropriate discriminant to the key on which the entries are sorted into alphabetical order, so that the entries in English will appear together in one alphabetical sequence, followed, in separate sequences, by the entries for the respective languages. Separate sequences of Latin, Greek, and so on not only would provide for some special inquiries into his language but also would ensure that the frequency counts for words in each language sequence were not contaminated by words from other languages (e.g. *chat/chât*).

Other Non-authorial Matter

Other material not by the author, like the stage directions in some texts of plays, extensive quotations, or identified portions of collaborative works, also is capable of distinction and separate listing by the addition of tags during pre-editing. Again, the main object is to purify the statistics. The general principle governing comprehensiveness is that the whole of a text attributed to an author should be concorded, but material which is alien to the author or his language should be reserved for separate listing.

Textual Variants

Textual variants introduce other complex technical problems together with enlarged possibilities that statistics will be contaminated. The inclusion of textual variants becomes an important consideration when an author's work exists in different versions (e.g. Wordsworth's 1805 and 1850 *Prelude*) or when there are two or more texts of independent authority which may each preserve the author's words (e.g. *Hamlet*). In addition, as for Shakespeare, there may be a long tradition of emendation in which a number of conjectures compete for acceptance. For the base text of the concordance, as has already been established, the concordance editor rests on the authority of the edition he has chosen. In that edition the editor of the text has solved problems of text as best he could and supplied a coherent linear text for concording. Most concordance editors are content to leave matters there. Nevertheless, there is sometimes a clear demand for a more extensive array of information. Editors are greatly helped by opportunities to consider the weight of particular conjectural emendations in relation to an array of passages in the author's works in which the same word occurs. However, there are several difficulties associated with the inclusion of textual variants and textual conjectures in concordances. Unless a variorum text prepared by a competent editor exists, the concordance editor will lack clear authority for the inclusion of the variants,[54] and the user of the concordance will not have a single established text to which to refer for the supplementary information which inevitably becomes necessary. Further, there may be problems of reference between an established text and the materials on which it depends, problems which also exist if two versions of a conflated text (the *Prelude,* for instance, although this is unlikely) were to be included in a single concordance. In addition, the variants cannot be included in the frequency counts: that would be to the detriment of the statistics. Nevertheless, some commentators would consider the exception irrelevant to the readings of collateral substantive texts. Furthermore, although the conjectures rejected by the editor of the base text, or some of them, may be included for listing in conjunction with contexts for the established readings, it is doubtful whether conjectures should be listed in the main sequence of HWs, and they should not figure in the frequency counts.

In the general area of the treatment of textual variants, the editor must be guided by the principles governing the construction of concordances which were discussed in the earlier chapters and take account of the points mentioned above. It is obvious enough that the practices which determine the treatment of the text of an author as copious as Shakespeare may be largely irrelevant to the concordance of an author whose works do not carry a similar burden of textual exegesis, but practical expedients in a particular case will depend considerably on

CHAPTER 6

STATISTICS

THE previous chapter has touched on many of the concerns of this heading. There is widespread agreement that concordances should provide statistics of some kind, although the kinds of figures and tables which should be made available in the published concordance are often not specified. The difficulty here is to determine the extent to which the concorder should provide the results of analysis beyond the materials on which subsequent analyses may depend. Nevertheless, consistency with the conception of the literary concordance as a general purpose tool recommends the conclusion that the concordance should provide those basic figures which allow the derivation of other statistics. In general one might accept demands for frequency counts for every item and type and token totals, probably in the form of a separate table which lists the n most common words in descending order of frequency. Notwithstanding, there are serious limitations inherent in the capture of lexical information by computer which need to be acknowledged before readers join in the general cry for bigger, better statistics. Sometimes it seems that statisticians are not overly concerned with what items are counted so long as they have figures for manipulation, yet common sense indicates that the most sophisticated statistical techniques can reveal nothing reliable about data which is contaminated.[55] The issue here is to determine what information is counted by the computer for publication in the concordance. In one concordance at least the figures count the contexts listed beneath the HWs rather than the occurrences of the words themselves.[56] Although Dr. Tallentire may claim that "the word is ... relatively unambiguously bounded for the computer (by the space and a small subset of orthographic symbols)..." (op. cit., pp. 41-2), in any particular concordance the HWs are complex, and the contexts listed underneath them — unless the concordance was lemmatised and homographs separately listed — will contain a variety of words which the HWs, and consequently their counts, misrepresent. Graphically, *might* n. and *might* v. are one word; grammatically, *gods* and *god's* (i.e. *god is*) are two words although counted together under a single HW; lexically, however, they are one word: the discussion of orthographic, graphemic, homonymic, and polysemantic homographs in chapter 3 shows how difficult it is to count words.

In short, although a statistician can scan the entries beneath each HW and refine the categories according to his understanding of "word", there is little point in providing a table of words in frequency of occurrence unless certain conditions have been met. (1) Old spellings should be listed under modern-spelling headings. (2) The modern-spelling HWs themselves should not admit spelling variation, i.e. there should be no mixture of English *honour* and American *honor* in the HWs, for example, and the MURDER/MURTHER kind of variation as in the Harvard Shakespeare concordance should be reduced. (3) For counting there should be no inconsistency amongst hyphenated and other compounds, e.g. SOME BODY, SOME-BODY, and SOMEBODY. (4) There must be consistent treatment of "words", particularly elisions, perhaps even lemmatization, and (5) correct distinction of homographs, with the exclusion of (6) non-authorial text, (7) extensive quotations, and (8) text in foreign languages. I know of no English concordance which meets these criteria although the impact of these matters on frequency counts is demonstrably significant. Professor Barron Brainerd notes that the counts of Elderton and Spevack for *2H4* show a difference of 426 words (types, not tokens), an error of 0.0166. The differences between the hand counts of Alfred Hart and the computer counts of the Spevack concordances are even more remarkable; for *2H6*, for example, it is just under 25%.[57]

The remarks above do not imply hostility towards counts, figures, or statistics; they have an assured place in linguistics. On the contrary, those who value the aid statistics can afford must insist that concordance editors resist the lure of the figures which the computer can pour forth with numerate but mindless ease, in favour of rigorous procedures designed to produce meaningful counts.[58]

CHAPTER 7

OTHER MATERIAL

AS WELL as statistical tables there are other accoutrements to the well-tempered concordance. Paramount amongst these is the editor's *Introduction* to which, many times, too little attention is given — both by the editor when he writes it and user of the concordance before he uses it. The editor must acknowledge his responsibility to describe and explain the organization and arrangement of the concordance and the limitations which may have been forced upon him by various local and wider circumstances. There is no more important part of the introduction than that which establishes the editor's choice of base text and his method of making it available for concording, but he must, to be brief, outline his position and procedures on all of the substantial topics discussed above.

Then there is a variety of *auxiliary tables* which might be provided to complement the main arrangement. Statistical tables apart, some editors include a table of the HWs sorted in reverse order, i.e. from the end of the word through to its beginning, which is useful for the study of some inflections and morphemes. Tables of rhymes can be compiled for poetry, and tables of frequency of publication. One can hardly limit the kind of supplementary material which imaginative concordance editors, heedful of the demands of their texts and the capabilities of the computer — not to mention the purses of the prospective purchasers — may print with the main concordance. Nor is it possible to establish, without consideration of the particular circumstances, the kind of supplementary information which the concordance editor must undertake as an essential part of his task.

CHAPTER 8

SPECIAL FORMS OF CONCORDANCE

IF THE virtue of the conventional concordance arrangement described in the preceding pages is that it will satisfy the greater proportion of inquiries addressed to the concordance with relative ease and promptness, its principal deficiency is that it will not readily provide for a host of more specialized — and on that account, potentially more valuable — approaches to language and literature. I have suggested that, since specialization is achieved at the cost of a constricted domain of potential use, a concordance directed at the largest number of users will suit most authors. Nevertheless, there is a wide range of alternative concordance arrangements to accommodate a variety of special applications which can always usefully supplement a general concordance and for which the stature of the author — as with the *Complete and Systematic Concordance to the Works of Shakespeare* — may sometimes justify publication. In the main, however, special concordances are analytical instruments for specialized investigations, and publication is rarely the principal aim of their execution.

Although the design of special concordances is limited only by the needs and imagination of the investigator and special concordances need have no common characteristics, it is useful to examine briefly a number of examples already mentioned in the literature for what they reveal of the current concerns of scholars and of possibilities for future development of concordances. In some instances the arrangement of the special concordance differs little from that of the general concordance: only the addition of special kinds of information, or the provision of information conventionally omitted (like the high-frequency less-significant words) marks the specialized function of the concordance. Usually the special concordance will be preceded by a general concordance, either as the preliminary stage in the preparation of the special concordance, or as a separate earlier publication, perhaps by another editor. The alphabetical array of entries will allow the concordance editor to identify special entries and to add discriminants for resorting (for a lexicon, for example) into a special, sometimes non-alphabetical arrangement. There are many possibilities, but almost invariably a general concordance is a valuable instrument in the creation of a special concordance.

Grammatical Concordance

Dr. Dolores Burton used a "grammatical" concordance during the writing of her *Shakespeare's Grammatical Style, a computer-assisted analysis of Richard II and Antony and Cleopatra* (Austin, University of Texas Press, 1973); the epithet refers to the kind of use to which the concordance was fitted rather than a significant attribute of the concordance itself.[59] In a sense the grammatical concordance is the converse of the conventional concordance, for the function words commonly represented by summary counts of frequency, or line references and counts only — the articles, pronouns, and prepositions, for instance — are in the grammatical concordance represented by full contexts. One might expect in a published concordance of this kind to find that the non-functional words (in terms of a special syntactical definition) were suppressed or only summarily represented, and that there was a certain amount of distinction and subordination of the entries in order to reveal the peculiar functions of each HW. In any event, in such a concordance the contexts would themselves require to be edited to represent a suitably comprehensive syntactical unit which would, ideally, enable the user to examine the relation of the function word to its context without recourse to the text from which the concordance entries were drawn.

Cluster Concordance

Another special concordance arrangement was suggested by

Demetrius J. Koubourlis in a paper delivered at a computer conference in Los Angeles in 1975.[60] He observed that lemmatic dispersion, the distribution of different forms of a single lexical item (e.g. *sing, sang, sung*), throughout the conventional concordance alphabet was particularly great when the source language was highly inflectional. Although there is no great problem in English, for such languages as Russian or Welsh which are both pre- and post-inflected, the concordance user must remember to consult a number of places in the concordance sequence when his concern is to collect all available information about a single lexical item. One solution to the problem of dispersion is the dictionary (discussed in Chapter 3), but since the dictionary arrangement is rather the product of lexical analysis than a tool designed to facilitate it, there is virtue in a stage which falls between the conventional non-lemmatized concordance and the dictionary: it is the cluster concordance.

This arrangement is named from the way in which forms of the same lemma "cluster" around the lemma or "alphabetic point of reference" if the concordance editor follows the procedures which Dr. Koubourlis advocates in his paper. The three variant arrangements of Fig. 7 show the intermediary nature of the cluster concordance and its usefulness for lexical analysis.

CONVENTIONAL	CLUSTER	DICTIONARY
SANG	SANGUINE	SANGUINE
SANGUINE	SEA	SEA
SEA	SINEW	SINEW
SINEW	SANG	SING
SING	SING	SANG
SINGING	SINGING	SINGING
SINGLE	SINGS	SINGS
SINGS	SUNG	SUNG
SON	$SINGLE_1$ (*v.*)	$SINGLE_1$ (*v.*)
SUN	$SINGLE_2$ (*n.*)	$SINGLE_2$ (*n.*)
SUNG	SON	SON
SUNLIGHT	SUN_1 (*v.*)	SUN_1 (*v.*)
	SUN_2 (*n.*)	SUN_2 (*n.*)
	SUNLIGHT	SUNLIGHT

Fig. 7. Showing arrangement of HWs in conventional, cluster, and dictionary-form concordances (adapted from Koubourlis).

If it occurred that the lexical interest of an author's works was great enough to warrant the publication of a concordance in this intermediate form, the editor would provide references at the conventionally alphabetized point of reference to the location of the lemmatized form, e.g. "SUNG *see after* SINGING", or the like.

Bilingual Concordance

When a text exists in two languages, usually as the result of translation, it may be advantageous to examine the vocabulary of the translation in relation to that of the original work. Susan Hockey describes the results of an experiment on an analogous case, a work in Sanskrit translated into English and Russian where the aim was to compare the two translations.[61] It is always possible to concord each text separately using the techniques appropriate to the distinctive characteristics of each language, and then to compare the two concordances side by side. However, there will inevitably be differences between the order of HWs of the two concordances which will make comparisons inconvenient. As the examples which Susan Hockey provides show, the use of synonymous expressions will disturb the order of entries under HWs: the Russian text uses the appropriate word for *time* in the phrase (presumably) "for a time", whereas the English version has *temporarily*.

BALCON avoids such consequences by the simple device of printing two concordances. The base text for one concordance was the Russian version which was introduced to the programme line by line on alternative cards with the English version. During pre-editing, the words required to be concorded were identified in each text by specific tags. When the Russian text was concorded the context of the base text (Russian) was taken for sorting and printing together with the context of the associated English line. The converse process was followed for the English version. Finally, a concordance was printed in Cyrillic characters in order of the Russian headings, with contexts from and references to the Russian version accompanied in parallel on the right-hand side of the page by the English counterparts to the Russian contexts. Then the equivalent sequence was printed for the English version.

In programmes of this kind — any programme which must deal with two texts — often the greatest difficulty is to ensure the correct sequencing of the two texts. If the languages are very different in word order, or one language much more diffuse than the other, it may be very difficult, to the point of being impossible, to ensure that the alternative contexts contain the HW intended to be illustrated. It is probably correct that pre-editing will not cope with all such difficulties, and that for a published concordance post-editing, as I have earlier described, will be necessary in order to improve the contexts. In the future, programming devices may be found to enable a bilingual concordance to offer alternative contexts in a single sequence (rather than across the page), with the concorded word in the context aligned with the equivalent term in the other text. KWIC techniques, especially "wrap-around" contexts, may be usefully applied here.[62]

Character Concordance

A rather more specialized form of concordance is the "character concordance" in which the speeches in a play or a novel, for instance, which are attributed to a particular speaker in the text, are concorded separately from passages of text which are narrative or assigned to other speakers. Although the benefits of being able to examine how an author may use different kinds of language to characterize speakers are not difficult to conceive, the only English concordance which attempts such a function is Dr. Marvin Spevack's *Complete and Systematic Concordance to the works of Shakespeare,* to which I have already referred from time to time. Character concordances should be accompanied, as Dr. Spevack's is, by a complete concordance to the whole text, since the relationship of characters to the general linguistic milieu is intrinsically interesting.

In general, character concordances do not differ greatly from the conventional concordance. Dr. Spevack identifies speeches in prose or verse and supplies appropriate statistics of speeches, which may be subjected to different kinds of statistical analysis. In such a concordance it may be valuable to identify the character to whom a particular speech is addressed, when that is appropriate, and to particularise asides or *sotto voce* speeches and the like, but by and large there is not much more information than this which might be provided.

Master Concordance

The following two types of concordance are comprehensive. Dr. Louis Ule refers to the "master concordance" not as a realized but rather as a projected conception:

> "A master concordance of a particular literary group, say, the Elizabethans, would list all the words used by all the authors in the group and, after each word entry, the names of the authors who use the word and the frequency of use by each author".[63]

The problems of amalgamating words and frequency lists for a number of authors are not insuperable, especially if those records were prepared on magnetic tape in a common format. However, there are serious difficulties, as Dr. Ule himself points out, which arise from the topics discussed in previous chapters: variant practices of spelling, hyphenation, treatment of material in foreign languages, collaborative works, and marginalia result in inconsistencies amongst different concordances which seriously undermine the usefulness of the statistics which could be derived from a master concordance. In this respect a master concordance may prove harmful, since, unless it was edited to a rigorous standard, the comfortable array of statistics would serve to conceal the different practices of the contributing original concordances and support an unjustifiable confidence in the statistical calculations derived from that data.

Many of these objections might be met by master indexes to concordances, especially an index which could be updated from time to time and therefore might best be maintained on magnetic tape. The distinction I wish to assert involves the omission of the frequencies: a master index would merely advise the user that a certain word occurred in the canon of a particular author. The user would then consult the concordance where he would not only find statistics but also, from the contexts supplied beneath every heading, undertake the appropriate distinction of homographs and meanings. An index would be most valuable for unusual or rare words which are significant for lexico-graphical and literary studies. On the other hand, Dr. Ule's conception of a master concordance could also be adopted for a relatively small group of high-frequency words which are important to establish the position of a particular author's work within the statistical domain of the language of a period but for which the figures are not greatly subject to the distortions of homography, words like *a, the, I, me.* Some kind of comprehensive concordance becomes increasingly necessary as the number of existing concordances continues to grow.

Variorum Concordance

The best example of a "variorum" concordance, one to which I have already referred in different contexts (see especially p. 11) is the Ingram-Swaim Milton concordance which was not based on any modern edition of the poems but supplies a concordance to the texts of Milton's poems published mainly during his lifetime and to some authoritative manuscripts. The analogy is to a variorum edition which records the readings of a number of editors or commentators: the variorum concordance indexes the readings of a number of textual authorities. The crucial consideration here is not one of methodology — although certain technical matters will require close attention — but of selection of the material to be concorded. Selection cannot be avoided when an author like Milton or Shakespeare has an extensive textual history. There are three main categories of material to be considered: since an elaborate analysis of them would require a detailed account of the principles of textual criticism, a few observations must suffice.

First are the readings of authoritative texts, and authoritative text being in general terms one which depends closely on a manuscript or typescript of the author, or which demonstrates his direct concern with his text. For many authors authoritative texts are identified by bibliographers and editors, and the concordance editor may rely upon their investigations and the common consensus: there should not be much scope here for judgement and error. The authoritative texts will usually supply the concordance editor's base texts if there is no generally accepted critical text of definitive pretensions. The second category of textual material is the emendations which editors have made to the authoritative texts, corrections which restore sense and the "author's intentions". However correct and necessary emendations may appear (like *that* for *thst*), and through the passage of time acceptable to most readers, they lack authority: in a variorum concordance emendations should be distinguished for the information of the user. It is tempting to assert that the original reading should be restored or noted, but very often original readings are meaningless, like the example above, and their preservation would contribute little more than nonsense to the concordance. The concordance editor must of necessity exercise his judgement here and expose himself to criticism. Finally, there are the conjectures of editors which were not preferred in the text itself but relegated to textual or footnotes. Conjectures range from the sublime to the ridiculous, but not every reader will agree which is which. The concordance editor has little option but to identify the editions which will supply the conjectures (and emendations) to the variorum concordance and then concord every such reading. It would be disastrous to a user's confidence in the concordance if the concordance editor decided to pick and choose amongst the readings and conjectures of a particular edition. Many such difficulties are resolved if an author already has a variorum edition which the concordance editor can use as his base text and guide for the selection of editions published after the variorum. By and large a variorum concordance is the most demanding kind of work that can be contemplated by a prospective concordance editor; it is not remarkable that few concordances do more than take a few tentative steps in the direction of the variorum concordance.

CHAPTER 9

CONCLUSION

IN THE previous chapter the brief survey of special kinds of concordances to which reference is made in the literature beckoned towards areas of greater and greater complexity. It is true, of course, that if one wishes to undertake sophisticated enterprises, the problems one will encounter will be correspondingly complex. For computer-aided concordances this complexity is enhanced by the complexity of the technology adopted in order to accomplish the task: often more attention is given to the demands of the "labour-saving" device than to catering for the special requirements of the concordance form. Not-withstanding the arcane complexities amongst which the present discussion has wandered from time to time, the *essential* form of the concordance is simple. Its execution is equally simple. Recently many concordance editors have lost sight of that fact and, lusting for novelties, have abandoned the simplicities which they never really understood in the first place. I have tried here to explain why the traditional or conventional concordance — and these are not perjorative terms — assumes its present form, so that when a modern concordance editor undertakes to depart from it, he will do so after consideration, on a rational basis. On the other hand, when he does leave the comfortable simplicities of the usual concordance arrangement, the concordance editor often encounters complexities which may baffle him if he is inexperienced and lacks the hardihood to compensate for his unfamili-arity with concordances and computers. Again, I provide here some indication of the kinds of problems which are likely to arise and some means to cope with them, although, since a proliferation of complexities leads inevitably towards abstractions remote from the realities with which the prospective concordance editor hopes to deal, I have not elaborated the problems of concordance making as fully as I might have done.

I have discussed the general theory of concordances rather more fully than any other source known to me. Yet I hope this book can serve a practical end. Anyone who intends to prepare a concordance will, I hope, find it valuable, after he has made himself familiar with every important aspect of the texts which he intends to concord, to re-read the central parts of my argument as if it provided a checklist of the practical matters with which every concordance editor need concern himself. Depending again on the characteristics of his texts, he will find that I have dealt with every general question about which the concordance editor must come to a determination. Unless he considers the points mentioned here, his concordance will not be adequate.

Finally, a word about the form of publication, to which the concordance editor — and certainly the user — will not be indifferent. In the main, form of publication is an "accidental", like the make of computer by which a concordance is compiled, which I did not intend to discuss. Nevertheless, there are two general tendencies in the publication of concordances which need to be noted. Micropublication is as good a way of burying a concordance as I know of: editors who accept publication on microfiche or the like are content to see their works perish so long as they do not. A concordance is a reference book which, when it is used, is used intensively. It must be consulted in conjunction with other references, e.g. the base text, and the concordance is usually consulted at many different points in the alphabetical arrangement in quick succession. Micropublication does not permit comfortable, conventional use of a concordance; I have heard no good argument why scholarly users of concordances should adapt detrimentally to an inferior and marginally useful form of publication.

On the other hand, there is now very little excuse for publishing from computer printout. Concordance editors will seek to avoid that in any event since it is difficult to ensure the clear legibility of the print, even when the availability of upper- and lower-case print chains enables the concordance editor to avoid having to print the concordance entirely in the upper case characters so often and justifiably criticized by reviewers. Between these two modern extremes and the lavish but prohibitively costly type composition of earlier days lies photo-composition. Phototypesetting from magnetic tapes provided by the concordance editor is now as inexpensive as scholarly publication of this kind can reasonably be expected to be, and the concordance editor should not hesitate to recommend it to a prospective publisher, especially as the concordance editor will save the publisher much editorial expense by delivering a tape already edited for the photo-composition programme. However, as early as possible the concordance editor should determine the format in which the concordance will be published, because, unfortunately, sometimes form does determine content. Selection of format and type size, for instance, will affect the extent of the various fields assigned to context and text references, and the editor will seek to use the appropriate typographical devices to distinguish heading words and the like. Attention to those characteristics of the published concordance which will assist the user to consult the concordance productively is the final necessary attribute of the accomplished concordance editor.

THE COCOA CONCORDANCE PACKAGE

by ROBERT L. OAKMAN

A SCHOLAR today finds that his university computer centre has some kind of "canned" concordance programme available for his use. These vary widely in their features and suitability for literary texts. The COCOA programme package, developed at the Atlas Computer Laboratory in Britain (its acronym stands for Count and Concordance generation on Atlas) provides an excellent example of a well-conceived, general-purpose programme of wide literary applicability.[64] Incorporating features of several earlier concordance programmes, COCOA's authors stressed three major considerations in their design: making the programme machine-independent so that it could be run on different types of computers; setting it up so that literary users unfamiliar with the workings of a computer could use it; and including an array of flexible alternative features within the programme itself. Successful on all counts, the designers of COCOA have seen it adopted successfully throughout the world. Oxford University Computing Service has now taken over maintenance of COCOA and in early 1978 began plans to revise, update, and improve the programme without sacrificing any of its commendable, original characteristics.[65]

To allow COCOA to be machine-independent, its developers wrote it in the USASI Standard FORTRAN programming language, a basic version of the language acceptable on all computers that run FORTRAN. Since FORTRAN is the most common computer language in the world, COCOA has become internationally transportable and implemented on such machines as IBM 360/360, CDC 6600/7600, ICL System 4 and

1900 series, Digital Equipment PDP-10, Honeywell 635, and UNIVAC 1110. Along with the package comes a user's manual describing the optional features of the programme, the control cards that make it run, and numerous illustrative examples for the computer novice to see what COCOA can do.[66] Although the descriptions in the current COCOA user's manual are explicit, many scholars have found the control options of the programme, prepared for the computer on punchcards, cumbersome to use and susceptible to error because of the rigid, exacting detail of their formulae. The revision intends to make the control cards easier to use by replacing the complicated formulaic instructions by self-explanatory commands in simple English words. As before, a readable instruction manual with numerous examples is promised.

Apropos the kinds of decisions that the maker of a computer concordance must face, outlined in detail by Dr. Howard-Hill, the designers of COCOA considered wisely and made provisions within their programme to handle many of the sticky problems. For instance, the COCOA user can decide whether the programme is to treat hyphenated compound words singly or as two words in the index. He prepares the appropriate control cards and the programme acts accordingly. If the scholar wishes COCOA to list homographs as separate forms (for instance, MIGHT as both noun and verb), he can add suffixes to the different forms as he encodes (such as spelling the noun from MIGHT$_1$ and the verb MIGHT$_2$). By proper control declaration, the computer will collect the forms separately and yet suppress the numeral suffixes in the final printed concordance. Similarly, accents in foreign words can be preserved in the input text (ROUE for *wheel* and ROUE/ for *rake*) and still be aligned next to each other in proper alphabetical order in the word list (both preceding ROUER). The user has great freedom in defining his own alphabetical order so that, for example, the initial consonant clusters *ch* and *ll* in Spanish (as in *churro* and *llano*) can be considered separate letters and placed in the alphabetical word list behind all the words starting with *c* and *l*, respectively. The editor even has the option of marking various word forms such as parts of the verb *to be* (*is, are, was, were,* etc.) with a special symbol on input so that the machine will group all of them together in the index under the base form (in this case, *be*). In fact,

COCOA with its several flexible options can greatly assist the scholar in making editorial decisions about his texts prior to encoding in order that the result will be a readable and useful reference tool.

Input and output conventions of COCOA, likewise, offer the user considerable leeway in his choices. The programme accepts any unit of text chosen by the editor — line of verse, speech of a character in a drama, or sentence from a novel, for example. Regardless of its length, this unit becomes one logical record for computer storage with an appended identifier enclosed in angle brackets to mark location or source. Within the brackets the editor may typically want to include author, title, page, line, chapter, act, scene, etc., to break up his material into contextual units for later listing under each concordance entry. Only the first record of running text need be labelled in brackets upon input; the programme automatically aligns successive units accordingly. With this method of text identification within categories, the editor can then request selective indexes in addition to a full concordance. He might want to inspect only the words in the first act of a play; with proper control cards he instructs the computer to limit its search only to those text records.

The standard COCOA format for presentation of context under alphabetically ordered keywords is the KWIC variety with the keyword centrally aligned on the printed page. If preferred, the first word of the context record can be left-aligned, irrespective of the location of keyword within the record. As Howard-Hill has noted, some people object to KWIC presentation of context; yet the wide adoption of COCOA for both prose and verse in a spectrum of language suggests its acceptance by many scholars for their purposes. The computer can even alphabetize the context either to the left or the right of the centrally printed keyword; with this option, recurring sequences of several words, such as poetic formulae in Old English, show up clearly lumped together under each indexed word. Normally COCOA will produce results on a printer, but alternatively machine-readable output can be provided for later submission to photocomposition equipment when required.

Other strong inducements recommending COCOA as a more than adequate concordance package are the variety of auxiliary indexes and specialized searches the programme can produce with proper control cards. Besides concordances for full or selected segments of text already discussed, COCOA can routinely generate word frequency lists in alphabetical order, in frequency order from high to low number of occurrences, and in alphabetical order of their endings (all the words ending in -*ing* or -*ly* would appear together). Alphabetical listing by endings, useful for studying rhyme patterns and morphology in inflected languages, is also an available ordering for the entries of the main concordance. The programme's additional features for doing selective searches make it much more than a standard concordance package. The user can specify that he wants the machine to index only those keywords found within the following categories: a specific alphabetical range (for instance, only words beginning with *M, N,* or *O*), a frequency range (only words occurring above or below a certain frequency threshold), and inclusion or exclusion on a list prepared ahead of time by the editor. Additionally the programme can be instructed to look for words with particular endings or letter patterns (such as all words ending in -*ed* or all three-letter words). Indeed, COCOA's auxiliary indexes and searching capabilities virtually transform a basic concordance package into a general text-analysis programme.

Because of all of its features and options for handling word forms, text segments, concordance production, and selective searches, it is not surprising that COCOA has been widely adopted for numerous literary investigations with the computer. The continuing evolution of COCOA represents a serious commitment on the part of its developers to see what kinds of jobs, related to the concordance process, literary scholars want done; to write their programmes in a universal version of the popular FORTRAN language; and to explain how to use them in a readable manual generously supplied with illustrative examples. That the academic community appreciates their work is evidenced by the wide acceptance of COCOA throughout the world.

NOTES

1. It is worthwhile mentioning even as early as this that the prospective concordance editor who expects the computer to relieve him of all drudgery is self-deluded. Most often the use of the computer in linguistic enterprises substitutes one kind of drudgery for another.

2. Professor Marvin Spevack's *Complete and Systematic Concordance to the Works of Shakespeare*, Hildesheim, G. Olms, 1968-70, 6 vols., is a good example of a concordance which provides public access to both the conventional concordance arrangement (in vols. IV-VI) and a specialized arrangement of the text under the names of the speakers in each play (vols. I-III).

3. By Joseph Raben (The death of the handmade concordance, *Scholarly Publishing* 1 (1969) 61-9) quoting Ione Dodson Young's observation in the preface to her concordance to Byron's poetry — on which she laboured for 25 years — that her work was likely to be "the last of the handmade concordances".

4. *Dewey Newsletter* 1 (1967) 2.

5. Andrew Crosland, (ed.), *A Concordance to the Complete Poetry of Stephen Crane*, Detroit, Mich., Gale Research Co., 1975; Herman Baron (ed.), *A Concordance to the Poems of Stephen Crane*, Boston, G.K. Hall, 1974.

6. The concordancer's procedure in such a case is discussed on pp. 10-12.

7. See T. H. Howard-Hill, Toward a Jonson concordance: a discussion of texts and problems, *Research Opportunities in Renaissance Drama* XV-XVI (1972-3) 17.

8. Ibid., see pp. 12-13 for discussion of pre-editing and amalgamation with the base text of auxiliary textual materials.

9. A concordance to Swift's poetry [review], *Computer and the Humanities* 7 (1973) 219.

10. This is the procedure adopted in preparation of the definitive edition of Faulkner's works; see J. B. Meriwether, A proposal for a CEAA edition of William Faulkner, in *Editing Twentieth Century Texts*, (ed. Francess G. Halpenny, Toronto, Toronto UP, 1972), pp. 12-27.

11. Howard-Hill, op. cit., p. 19; I discuss the principal characteristics of such a concordance in relation to Jonson in the same place, *passim.*

12. *A Concordance to Milton's English Poetry* (ed. by William Ingram and Kathleen Swaim), (Oxford, Clarendon Press, 1972), p. v.

13. *A Concordance to the Writings of William Blake* (ed. by David B. Erdman), Ithaca, NY, Cornell UP, 1967.

14. "Heading word" (HW) is preferred to "lemma" as a neutral term denoting simply the "word" or form which stands at the head of an entry in a concordance. HWs correspond to Herdan's "types".

15. I shall ignore the case where hyphen sorts between R and S in the code of the Honeywell 635; special procedures not governed by the following principles are required.

16. See S. M. Parrish, Problems in computer concordances, *Studies in Bibliography* XV (1962) 6.

17. Cornell Blake, op. cit., p. xii. The HW occurs after CORNERS in correct alphabetical sequence as if the hyphen had been suppressed in the sort key.

18. See T. H. Howard-Hill, The Oxford old-spelling Shakespeare concordances, *Studies in Bibliography* XXII (1969) 154-6, for a fuller description of this procedure.

19. References are discussed more fully on pp. 26-7.

20. See Alan Markman, A computer concordance to medieval texts, *Studies in Bibliography XVII* (1964) 55-75, especially pp. 67-9 for discussion of references with spelling variants.

21. D. J. Koubourlis, From a word-form concordance to a dictionary-form concordance, in International Conference on Computers in the Humanities, University of Minnesota, 1973. *Computers in the Humanities* (ed. by J. L. Mitchell), Edinburgh, Edinburgh UP, 1974, pp. 225-33.

22. A further distinction — that of words like *good, better, best* and forms of the verb *to be* which are morphemically dissimilar in part but are lexically related — will be considered under "Lemmatization".

23. As William Ingram observes in Concordances in the seventies, *Computers in the Humanities* **9** (1974) 277.

24. Markman (op. cit., p. 69) and Koubourlis (op. cit., p. 231) each refer to the "dead end" of ambiguity.

25. Koubourlis, op. cit., p. 225. The "dictionary form" is the infinitive for verbs, the nominative singular for nouns, adjectives, etc.

26. Barnet Kottler and A. Markman (eds.), *A Concordance to Five Middle English Poems* . . . (Pittsburgh, Pittsburgh UP, 1966).

27. The Ingram-Swaim Milton concordance (op. cit.) uses an order the basis of which is not explained and is not easily deducible. *Paradise Lost* and *Paradise Regained* are followed by *Samson Agonistes* and a host of lesser works in no apparently mnemonic order; perhaps length determined the order.

28. Caroline Spurgeon *Shakespeare's Imagery and what it Tells Us*, Cambridge, Cambridge UP, 1965 (1st edn. 1935), pp. 195-9.

29 J. E. G. Dixon, A prose concordance: Rabelais, *ALLC Bulletin* **2** (1974) 47-54. Contexts are also discussed briefly by another compiler of a prose concordance in Andrew T. Crosland, The concordance and the study of the novel, *ALLC Bulletin* **3** (1975) 190-6.

30. An attempt to solve the problem of size, which arises from length of the original work as much as from the contexts, is the publication on microfiche of a word index together with the complete text of the concorded work; see Sibyl Jacobson, Robert Dilligan, and Todd K. Bender, *Concordance to Joseph Conrad's "Heart of Darkness"*, Carbondale, Ill., Southern Illinois UP, 1974; see also Crosland, op. cit., p. 190.

31. Dr. Dixon establishes "two fundamental requirements" for a context: "(1) it must be long enough to show the contextual matter of the key word; (2) it must be brief enough to be taken in at a glance." In the first point "contextual matter" is equivalent to "context"; the point is a tautology: what I think Dr. Dixon means is that the context must be long enough to satisfy some criterion. He defines the purpose of the citation later: "it is to show whether, and where, the author treats of a particular idea, concept, theme, situation, image, etc." I regard this as a burden to be placed on the context which is essentially insupportable for the conventional published concordance. Nevertheless, he believes that such a concordance must be short enough to reveal its significance at a glance, another impossibility which is perhaps an enthusiastic hyperbole on the author's part. And of course, the two requirements are essentially incompatible.

32. There is no need for me to labour the point as I have commented on the practice — which in my opinion is detrimental to the use of Dr. Spevack's important concordance — in another place: see T. H. Howard-Hill, The bard in chains, an examination of the *Harvard Concordance to Shakespeare, Costerus* **4** (1975) 107-22.

33. Roy A. Wisbey in an important, pioneering article (Concordance making by electronic computer, some experiences with the 'Wiener Genesis', *Modern Language Review* **57** (1962) 161-72) refers to pre-editing procedures adopted by Father Roberto Busa for the *Thesaurus Linguae Latinae* to produce common extended lexicographic contexts (pp. 165 f.). Pre-editing for contexts is usually combined with pre-editing for other purposes.

34. As observed by F. de Tollenaere, The problem of the context in computer-aided lexicography, in A. J. Aitken [and others] (eds.), *The Computer and Literary Studies*, Edinburgh, Edinburgh UP, 1973, p. 25.

35. The fullest discussion of the context-abstraction algorithm occurs in the introduction to the *Harvard Concordance to Shakespeare*, pp. vii-viii, which reprints similar information from the *Complete and Systematic Concordance* (as cited), vol. 4.

36. Tollenaere, op. cit., p. 29. This paper gives a comprehensive survey of the problem of contexts for lexicography.

37. The procedure I suggest assumes a computer method in which the messages which contain the individual items abstracted from the base text include the contexts as well as references to the base text in the computer. That is, the method does not assume that the whole concordance corpus exists in the computer (in main store, disc, or drum) at once, for direct access from index entries.

38. See the discussion in relation to foreign languages on pp. 59-60.

39. R. L. Widmann, *Shakespeare Quarterly* **14** (1973) 340.

40. One must distinguish, nevertheless, between sigla which are convenient for the purposes of computation and those which are convenient in a published concordance. If it suits him, the editor can label the different works "1, 2, ... *n*" according to the order in which he wants their entries to sort, just so long as he expands the sigla from a look-up table, in the output intended for publication.

41. H. H. Kleinman's review of Robert C. Williams, *A Concordance to the Collected Poems of Dylan Thomas*, Lincoln, Neb., Nebraska UP, 1967, in *Computers and the Humanities* **4** (1970) 275.

42. Kato, op. cit., p. 276. Frequency counts are discussed more specifically on p. 48.

43. H. P. Luhn, Keyword-in-context index for technical literature (KWIC index), *American Documentation* **11** (1960) 288-95; the system is described in IBM Form E20-8091 (1962), "Keywood-in-context (KWIC) indexing". A comprehensive analysis of and guide to KWIC indexes, including their literary uses, is Lucille H. Campey, *Generating and Printing Indexes by Computer*, ASLIB Occasional Publication, No. 11, London, Aslib, 1972.

44. In some KWOC concordances the indexed term is replaced in the context by asterisks in an unsightly manner. The character spaces freed by the deletion of the keyword may be taken up by an extended context.

45. Campey, op. cit., p. 10.

46. Second-field sorting is described in Earl D. Bevan, A Shaw concordance, *Modern Drama* **14** (1971) 164.

47. Marvin Spevack. Concordances: old and new, *Computer Studies in the Humanities & Verbal Behaviour* **4** (1) (1973) 17-19.

48. The Harvard Shakespeare concordance omits the contexts for 43 words which are,

nevertheless, available in the *Complete and Systematic Concordance.*

49. As Spevack, op. cit., p. 18, mentions.

50. *Harvard Concordance to Shakespeare*, p. v.

51. Reviewing Dr. Eric Domville's concordance to Yeats's plays, I commented on the presentation of 70 words by frequency counts alone: "The summarily-represented words should not be regarded as 'non-significant' as the editor writes but merely as words which are so frequent in the text that the ordinary user would receive no advantage from using the concordance to locate them; economy not significance determines their omission" (*University of Toronto Quarterly* **42** (1973) 426). There my view was consistent with Dr. Spevack's practice in the Harvard concordance. Now I assert that economy alone should not prevail in the selection or words for omission of contexts.

52. See H. H. Kleinman, Dylan Thomas: a work of words [Review of Robert Coleman Williams, *A Concordance to the Collected Poems of Dylan Thomas*, Lincoln, 1967], *Computers in the Humanities* **4** (1970) 277.

53. See Robert L. Oakman, Concordances from computers: a review article, *Proof* 3 (1973) 418.

54. "Authority" on p. 7 contains further comments relevant to this question.

55. D. R. Tallentire, Towards an archive of lexical norms, an appeal, *The Computer and Literary Studies*, (ed. by A. J. Aitken and others), Edinburgh, Edinburgh UP, 1973, pp. 39-60, gives a well-informed discussion on the value of statistics for stylistic and linguistic studies, which is, nevertheless, somewhat prone to the criticism above.

56. Eric Domville's Yeats concordance; see my *UTQ* review cited in ref. 51, p. 426.

57. The computer in statistical studies of William Shakespeare, *Computer Studies in the Humanities & Verbal Behaviour* **4** (9-15), (1973) 12.

58. Peter Davison reviewing *The Harvard Concordance to Shakespeare* (*The Library*, fifth series **29** (1974) 472-5) offers salutary warnings about that "very statistical precision which, paradoxically, is dangerous . . ." (p. 475).

59. For the fullest description of the grammatical concordance and its applications, see D. M. Burton, Some uses of a grammatical concordance, *Computers and the Humanities* **2** (4) (March 1968) 145-54.

60. "The cluster concordance and computer-aided lemmatization."

61. Susan M. Hockey, The bilingual analytical literary and linguistic concordance — BALCON, *ALLC Bulletin* **3** (2) (1975) 133-5.

62. A "wrap-around" context is one in which usually the context has a determined field, the keyword is printed in a prescribed position, often the middle of the context field, and words from the end of the context which could not be contained within it are "wrapped-around" and so appear at the beginning of the context field, e.g. *Pope's poem, "The RAPE of the Lock", Alexander.*

63. Master concordances, *ALLC Bulletin* **1** (2) (1973) 3-6, p. 3.

64. For a description, see Godelieve L. M. Berry-Rogghe and T. D. Crawford, Developing a machine-independent concordance program for a variety of languages, in *The Computer and Literary Studies* (ed. A. J. Aitken, R. W. Bailey, and N. Hamilton-Smith), Edinburgh, Edinburgh UP, 1973, pp. 309-16.

65. A series of articles, "The Oxford Concordance Project", describing a replacement for COCOA, which is being funded by a British government grant, will appear in the *Bulletin of the Association for Literary and Linguistic Computing* in 1979. Inquiries about the current state of COCOA and its successor should be addressed to Mrs. Susan Hockey, Oxford University Computing Service, 13 Banbury Road, Oxford OX2 6NN, England.

66. Godelieve L. M. Berry-Rogghe and T. D. Crawford, *COCOA: A Word Count and Concordance Generator*, Chilton, Didcot, Atlas Computer Laboratory, and Cardiff, Wales, University College, 1973.

BIBLIOGRAPHY

Concordances, A Selective Bibliography

(1) *General*

Ellis, Frederick S., Of concordance making, *Athenæum* **3379** (1892) 160; R. Black, ibid.
3380 (1892) 194; F. S. Ellis, ibid. **3381** (1892) 224. An illuminating correspondence
which is discussed by Howard-Hill, 1976, q.v.

Trimble, A. E., Concordance making in New Zealand, *Atlantic* **104** (1909) 364-7.

Cooper, Lane, The making and use of a verbal concordance, *Sewanee Review* **27** (2)
(1919) 188-206. Reprinted in his *Evolution and Repentance: mixed essays and
addresses*, Ithaca, NY, Cornell UP, 1935, pp. 18-53.

Fogel, Ephim G., Electronic computers and Elizabethan texts, *Research Opportunities
in Renaissance Drama* **5** (1960) 29-38. Revised in *Studies in Bibliography* **15** (1962)
15-31.

Parrish, Stephen M., Problems in the making of computer concordances, *Studies in
Bibliography* **15** (1962) 1-14.

Wisbey, Roy A., Concordance making by electronic computer; some experiences with
the 'Wiener Genesis', *Modern Language Review* **57** (2) (1962) 161-72. A pioneer
article, even more valuable than the preceding item.

Duggan, Joseph J., The value of computer-generated concordances in linguistic and
literary research, *Revue* **4** (1966) 51-60.

Hays, Davis G., Concordances, in *Introduction to Computational Linguistics*. New York
and London, 1967, pp. 170-9. Chiefly from the linguistic viewpoint.

Parrish, Stephen M., Computers and the muse of literature, in Bowles, Edmund A. (ed.),
Computers in Humanistic Research: readings and perspectives, Englewood Cliffs,
NJ, 1967, pp. 124-34.

Halporn, James H., The emperor's new clothes, *Revue* **4** (1969) 31-49. Interesting
reflections on the difficulties of using computers for humanistic purposes.

Raben, Joseph, The death of the handmade concordance, *Scholarly Publishing* **1** (1)
(1969) 61-9.

Parrish, Stephen M., Concordance-making by computer, its past, future, techniques and
applications, in Burelbach, Frederick M. (ed.) *Proceedings: Computer Applications
to Problems in the Humanities*. Brockport, NY, 1970, pp. 16-33.

Spevack, Marvin, Concordances, old and new, *Computer Studies in the Humanities and
Verbal Behaviour* **4** (1) (1973) 17-19.

Ingram, William, Concordances in the seventies, *Computers and the Humanities* **8** (5-6)
(1974) 273-7.

Crosland, Andrew T., The concordance and the study of the novel, *Association for
Literary and Linguistic Computing Bulletin* **3** (3) (1975) 190-6.

Howard-Hill, Trevor H., Of literary concordances, an early view, *ALLC Bulletin* **4** (3)
(1976) 215-20. On the exchange between Ellis and Black in 1892, q.v.

88   *Literary Concordances*

[object Object](2) *Particular, Mainly Technical*

Luhn, Hans P., Keyword-in-context index for technical literature (KWIC index), *American Documentation* 11 (4) (1960) 288-95. Reprinted in Hays, David G. (ed.), *Readings in Automated Language Processing*, New York, 1966, pp. 159-67. The origin of KWIC indexes.

Lamb, Sydney M. and Gold, Laura, *Concordances from Computers*, Berkeley, Calif., Mechanolinguistics project, University of California, 1964, 90 pp. diagrams (duplicated typescript). Concise account of three simple concordance routines.

Painter, J. A., Implications of the Cornell concordances for computing, in IBM Literary Data Processing Conference, 9-11 September, 1964, *Proceedings* (ed. by Jess B. Bessinger, Stephen M. Parrish, and Harry F. Arader), Yorktown Heights, NY, 1964, pp. 160-70.

Scharfenberg, K. F., P. H. Smith, and R. D. Villani, A concordance generator, *IBM Systems Journal* 3 (1) (1964) 104-11.

Smith, Philip H., A computer program to generate a text concordance, in IBM Literary Data Processing Conference, 9-11 September, 1964, *Proceedings* (ed. by Jess B. Bessinger, Stephen M. Parrish, and Harry F. Arader), Yorktown Heights, NY, 1964, pp. 113-27. Discusses Scharfenberg's concordance generator from the standpoint of the user.

Werner, Oswald, Systematized lexicography or ethnoscience: the use of computer made concordances, *American Behavioral Scientist* 10 (5) (1967) 5-8.

Burton, Dolores M., Some uses of a grammatical concordance, *Computers and the Humanities* 2 (4) (1968) 145-54.

Smith, Philip H., The state of the ICRH concordance generator, *ICRH Newsletter* 4 (5) (1969) 1-4.

Hines, Theodore C., Harris, Jessica L., and Levy, Charlotte L., An experimental concordance program, *Computers and the Humanities* 4 (3) (1970) 161-71.

Smith, O. Romaine, GENDEX: GENeral inDEXer of words with context, a concordance generator, *Computer Studies in the Humanities and Verbal Behavior* 3 (1) (1970) 50-3.

Hamilton-Smith, N., A versatile concordance program for a textual archive, *in* Wisbey, Roy A. (ed.) *The Computer in Literary and Linguistic Research,* Cambridge, 1971, pp. 235-44.

Campey, Lucille H., *Generating and Printing Indexes by Computer,* London, ASLIB, 1972, 101 pp., tables, 30 cm (ASLIB Occasional Publications, No. 11).

Farringdon, Michael G., The interactive interrogation of text and concordance files, in Aitken, A. J. (ed.), *The Computer and Literary Studies,* Edinburgh, 1973, pp. 317-24.

Berry-Rogghe, Godelieve L. M., COCOA, a word count and concordance generator. *ALLC Bulletin* 1 (2) (1973) 29-31.

Berry-Rogghe, Godelieve L. M. and Crawford, T. D., Developing a machine-independent concordance program for a variety of languages, in Aitken, A. J. (ed.), *The Computer and Literary Studies,* Edinburgh, 1973, pp. 309-16.

Tallentire, D. Roger, Towards an archive of lexical norms, a proposal, in Aitken, op. cit., pp. 25-35.

Tollenaere, F. de, The problem of the context in computer-aided lexicography, in Aitken, op. cit., pp. 25-35.

Ule, Louis, Master concordances, *ALLC Bulletin* 1 (2) (1973) 3-6.

Dixon, J.E.G. A prose concordance: Rabelais, *ALLC Bulletin* 2 (3) (1974) 47-54.

Koubourlis, Demetrius J., From a word-form concordance to a dictionary-form concordance, *in* Mitchell, J. L. (ed.), *Computers in the Humanities,* Edinburgh, 1974, pp. 225-33.

Hockey, Susan M. and Shibayev, V., The bilingual analytical and linguistic concordance — BALCON, *ALLC Bulletin* **3** (2) (1975) 133-9.

(3) *Specific Concordances*

Thomas, Ralph, Tennyson concordances, *Notes & Queries*, ser. 10, **11** (1909) 261-2; F. Jarratt, ibid., p. 353.

Strachan, Lionel R. M., Tennyson concordance of 1870, *Notes & Queries*, ser. 13, **1** (1923) 349.

Tatlock, John S. P., The Chaucer concordance, *Modern Language Notes* **38** (8) (1923) 504-6.

Parker, W. M., Shakespeare concordances, *Times Literary Supplement* 12 May 1945, p. 228. Useful survey of early concordances up to Bartlett.

Markman, Alan, A computer concordance to medieval texts, *Studies in Bibliography* **17** (1964) 55-75.

Siberz, Joseph K., and Devine, J. G., Computer-made concordances to the works of the early Christian writers, in IBM Literary Data Processing Conference, 9-11 September, 1964, *Proceedings* (ed. by Jess B. Bessinger, Stephen M. Parrish and Harry F. Arader), Yorktown Heights, NY, 1964, pp. 128-47.

Kottler, Barnet, and Markman, A., *A Concordance to Five Middle English Poems*, Pittsburgh, University of Pittsburgh Press, 1966. Particularly useful for the Preface (pp. vii-xxv) and the instructions for using the concordance (pp. xxvi-xxvii).

Howard-Hill, Trevor H., Shakespeare sought out by computation, *Shakespearean Research and Opportunities* **4** (1968-9) 103-16. Review article on the first volumes of the *Complete and Systematic Concordance to the Works of Shakespeare*.

Donow, Herbert S., Concordance and stylistic analysis of six Elizabethan sonnet sequences, *Computers and the Humanities* **3** (4) (1969) 205-8.

Howard-Hill, Trevor H., The Oxford old-spelling Shakespeare concordances, *Studies in Bibliography* **22** (1969) 143-64.

Marder, Louis, New Shakespeare concordances, *Shakespeare Newsletter* **20** (1-3) (1970) 8-10.

Bevan, Earl D., A Shaw concordance, *Modern Drama* **14** (12) (1974) 155-68.

Howard-Hill, Trevor H., Towards a Jonson concordance, a discussion of texts and problems, *Research Opportunities in Renaissance Drama* **15-16** (1972-3) 17-32.

Berger, Sidney, A method for compiling a concordance for a middle English text, *Studies in Bibliography* **26** (1973) 219-28.

Oakman, Robert L., Concordances from computers: a review article, *Proof* **3** (1973) 411-25.

Howard-Hill, Trevor H., The bard in chains, an examination of the *Harvard Concordance to Shakespeare*, *Costerus*, new ser. **4** (1975) 107-22.

GLOSSARY

ALTHOUGH the student of literature who intends to prepare a concordance will find many of the technical terms and concepts here familiar to him, it is quite likely that the computer programmer to whom he must explain his requirements, having a different technical vocabulary, will need to acquire this one. The glossary is useful, too, for quick reference, especially if the reader encounters a term unfamiliar to him in the discussion before it is formally introduced with a definition.

Accidentals. Strictly, formal characteristics of the text (like the size of type in which it is printed) which convey no significant information to a reader and which, therefore, an editor may vary.

Apheretic forms. Words like *'tween* which lack the initial syllable.

Aphetic forms. Words like *'gainst* or *'twill* which lack the initial character.

Base text. The text chosen for input from which the contexts are drawn and to which the text references refer.

Compounds. Words which are joined together through combination (*housemaid*), elision (*you're*) or hyphenation (*corn-field*).

Concordance. Alphabetical arrangement of words (types) in a text or number of texts, in which the use of each token (individual occurrence) is illustrated by a context and accompanied by a reference to the text and part of text from which it was drawn.

Concordance, bilingual. Concordance which concords a text in two languages in two separate sequences but with the heading words of one language illustrated by the corresponding contexts of the other language.

Concordance, canonical. A concordance to a standard or definitive edition of an author's complete works (or canon).

Concordance, character. A hypothetical kind of special concordance appropriate to dramatic works in which speeches are attributed in the concordance to the character in the play who speaks them, and also the character addressed may be identified.

Concordance, cluster. Dr. Demetrius J. Koubourlis identifies the cluster concordance as a special form which falls between the conventional concordance and the dictionary. (*See* Fig. 7.)

Concordance, grammatical. A term used by Dr. Dolores Burton in connection with a concordance in which the common function words of great syntactical importance are given full entries; words of high content may not be represented fully or at all in this special form of concordance.

Concordance, master. The amalgamation of a number of separately generated concordances which relate to a common period, genre, or the like, suggested by Dr. Louis Ule.

Concordance, textual. A concordance which takes account of the variants amongst different states of a literary work and the emendations and conjectures of editors.

Concordance, variorum. A special concordance which uses a base text but incorporates textual material from other sources, e.g. variant readings, emendations, and textual conjectures.

Concordance generator. A general computer programme like COCOA which, after the introduction of special values for certain variables, will produce a specific concordance programme for the user.

Conjectures. Suggested corrections of textual errors which are not inserted in the text.

Context. A quotation from the base text in which the concorded word occurs; the context is to identify the circumstances of the word's use, to greater or less amplitude.

Context, algorithmic. Contexts appropriate for every word in a text may be derived mechanically by the concordance programme by an algorithm which takes account of syntactical clues such as punctuation.

Context, fixed-length. Illustrative contexts which are confined in length to a specific number of characters (or space) in the published concordance, usually for economy.

Context, post-edited. Contexts which were examined after generation by the concordance programme and edited to illustrate the use of the word more exactly.

Context, pre-edited. The concordance editor introduces tag characters which delimit optimum contexts before the concordance programme is run.

Count only words. Words which for a variety of reasons but mainly for economy are not given contexts or separate entries in the concordance but are represented summarily by a frequency count. Such words are often *the, a, of, I, he.*

Dictionary. In relation to concordances, an arrangement of headings and entries which show lemmatization, conjugate forms being subordinated beneath a lemma. (*See also* **Lemma**).

Emendations. Editorial corrections inserted in a text.

Entries. The units of information beneath each heading-word which consist of the context, text reference, etc., as appropriate. (See also **Fields.**)

Fields. In the common published concordance entry, after the HW a single entry consists of (1) the *context*, (2) the concorded *word* within the context, (3) the sign which identifies the *text*, and (4) the *reference* to the specific part of the text. These fields should not be confused with the fields which a computer programmer may establish within the structure of the messages generated by the concordance programme, although they will occur in it.

Frequency counts. Totals of the number of instances of the concorded word in the entries listed beneath each HW are often supplied for each sequence of entries.

Heading word (HW). The word printed, usually with some kind of typographical distinction, at the head of a sequence of concordance entries which illustrate the occurrence of the grapheme. The use of a HW does not necessarily imply consistency of the ensuing entries or subordination of following headings. (*See also* **Lemma.**)

Homoform insensitivity. The "lumping together of homographic forms on the basis of spelling identity alone without taking phonological and semantic differences into account" (Koubourlis).

Homographs, graphemic. Forms which differ in shape (*god, god's, god'$[i]$s*) but are morphemically similar, being graphemes of a single morpheme (*god*).

Homographs, homonymic. Words which are graphemically similar (like *art/might/will* as nouns and verbs) but morphemically dissimilar: identical in spelling but different in origin and meaning.

Homographs, orthographic. Words like *do, doe, doo,* which are orthographically distinct forms of a single morpheme (*do*).

Homographs, polysemantic. Words like *act* which have several distinct meanings which are not distinguished by spelling.

Index verborum, *see* Verbal index.

KWIC indexes. *K*ey-*W*ord-*In*-*C*ontext indexes are commonly applied to the titles of technical literature to provide rudimentary subject indexing. KWIC indexes are a specialized variant of the common concordance. (*See* Fig. 6.)

KWIC, double. A variation of KWIC indexing in which the main concorded word is extracted and the remaining significant words are rotated (in a wrap-around field, q.v.) and displayed subordinately under the main term.

KWOC indexes. A form of KWIC index in which the keyword (HW) is printed *O*ut of *C*ontext at the left of the page at the head of the sequence of entries, as in the conventional concordance.

Lemma. The heading used in a dictionary in which the entries are lemmatized to any extent, that is, variant forms of words (like conjugations) subordinated in the arrangement to base forms, the lemmas. The usual lemma for a verb is the infinitive form, (e.g. *be*/*is*/*was*/*were*), whereas adjectives used in comparative constructions are listed beneath the lemma of the uncompared form (e.g. *good*/*better*/*best*).

Lexicon, *see* **Dictionary.**

Location only words. Words which, mainly for economy, are given text references (and frequency counts) but no contexts.

Orthography. Spelling and, less frequently nowadays, punctuation.

Post-editing. Inspection of the results of a concordance programme in order to make distinctions, etc., for a further computer run or for publication.

Pre-editing. Preparation of text to be concorded for input by the addition of specific instructions for the imput typist and/or tags or special characters to control the running of the concordance programme.

References. Inserted in the alphabetical sequence of HWs, references either lead the inquirer from where there is no information to where it is listed (*intreat* see *entreat*') or refers him to additional material elsewhere in the concordance in which he might be interested (*against* see also '*gainst*).

References, text. Text references supplied for every separate entry in a concordance allow the user to consult the base text from which the contexts were drawn. Text references may be to consecutively numbered typographical lines or to structural units of the work, like chapters and paragraphs, or acts and scenes, e.g. 3.2.126.

Sigla, text. Conventional abbreviations for the titles of literary texts adopted for the sake of economy and printed in the text reference field of the individual concordance entry, e.g. *FQ* for *Faerie Queene*.

Substantives. The meaning-bearing elements of a text; therefore the words and some punctuation.

Tags. Any characters or symbols inserted in a text during pre-editing to identify exceptional occurrences of textual phenomena which the computer programme could not otherwise identify.

Text, authoritative. In general a text which depends closely on a manuscript or typescript of the author, i.e. a text in the preparation of which the author himself participated directly or indirectly.

Text, base, *see* **Base text.**

Text reference field, *see* **Reference, text.**

Tokens. Individual occurrences of words in a passage of text which may be counted. (*See also* **Types.**)

Types. The different words which occur in a text in various numbers. In the sentence 'the fly ate the spider before the spider ate the fly' there are 5 types (the 4, fly 2, ate 2, spider 2, before 1): the tokens are counted.

Variants. Textual readings which distinguish one state of a text from another.

Verbal index. Alphabetical list of words in a text with references to where they may be found in the text (e.g. chapter 1, line 46) but no contexts.

Word-form diffusion. Characteristic of the concordance arrangement, in that markedly dissimilar conjugations of verbs (e.g. *do/did/done*), for example, are scattered throughout the alphabetic sequence of HWs rather than being subordinated to a lemma (Kourbourlis). (*See also* **Lemma.**)

Wrap-around context. Usually found in KWIC indexes, the wrap-around context is created when the keywords are centred on the page. Context which is pushed off the end of the entry is wrapped around and printed at the front of the context field — which is of fixed-length. (*See* Fig. 6.)

INDEX